The Power of a Parent's Blessing is a b
sage that will place your family relai
Jesus and His Word.

—Loren Cunningham
Founder of Youth With A Mission

The Power of a Parent's Blessing by Craig Hill is an absolute must-read for every parent. Craig reveals the difference between a life that has a parent's blessing versus one that does not. As in past books, Craig supports all his conclusions with Scripture. I urge you to read and apply what is contained in this book if you are a parent or are soon to be a parent.

—Os Hillman
Author of *TGIF Today God Is First* and *Change Agent*

It's been my honor to teach with and to listen to Craig Hill teach on the incredible power of a parent's blessing. Now he's captured his message in a book you *must* read. You'll discover why the blessing is so crucial for *your* child—and your life and relationships as well! And he's captured "take home now" specifics for the critical times you can step in and bless that son or daughter God has given you.

—John Trent, PhD
Coauthor of *The Blessing*
and president of StrongFamilies.com
and The Blessing Challenge (www.TheBlessing.com)

As the family of God it is absolutely vital that we tap into the power and significance of blessing within our families for "such a time as this." Craig Hill has a deep revelation of the true meaning of "blessing" and brings extreme hope and assurance that it is never too late to bless our children and future generations. Using real-life stories and his vast knowledge of the power of blessing, Craig helps us to embrace Father God's blessing over our lives and empowers us with practical help to impart it to our children.

Craig's teaching for the last twenty years has personally impacted our family. Twelve years ago we threw a huge blessing celebration for our oldest son based on the teaching about the bar barakah. We have done this for each of our children, and the favor of God that is clearly resting on each of them as young adults is beyond explanation.

We believe it can be attributed only to the grace of God and imparting His blessing to our children in a tangible way. To this day Craig plays a huge role in our lives, not only by building us up to minister to married couples around the world but also by sharing his continual wisdom in the area of blessing.

Craig is one of our closest friends and mentors, and we glean not only from his profound teaching but also from the exemplary way he lives out these truths in his own life.

This book is an excellent and engaging resource for individuals, parents, and ministers who truly desire to live out their limitless heritage as children of God. We look forward to giving this book to our children when they are married so they can understand the kingdom principles contained in it and be empowered to bless their own children. The seeds of blessing that we sow today will be reaped for generations to come!

—Bob and Audrey Meisner
Best-selling authors of *Marriage Under Cover*
and TV hosts of *My New Day*

As a parent I have always wanted the best for my children. I knew exactly how to provide for their physical and material needs but had no knowledge of how best to help them grasp their true value and purpose in life. This book provided not only a biblical basis for why blessing my children was that missing link but also a practical guide for how and when to do it.

I, like many parents, believed that just loving my children unconditionally was the best I could do, but I learned that loving them did not help them establish their identity or their destiny. Blessing them does that. My wife and I never experienced this from our parents, who never experienced it from theirs. The power of blessing has been lost to modern society.

We now bless our children on a frequent basis, which is the ultimate expression of our love for them. And here's the good news: it works! Imparting a blessing to our children is not a teaching. It is an experience that my wife, my children, and I now share together.

—SAM CASTER
Founder of Mannatech, Inc. and MannaRelief Ministries
Grand Prairie, Texas

Craig's new book, *The Power of a Parent's Blessing*, is the compilation of over twenty years of teaching and practical, real-life experience. If only every parent could grasp this simple but powerful concept of blessing their children, it would revolutionize their family relationships. As a pastor and father I have seen firsthand how the power of a parent's blessing has impacted our own family and the lives of so many others across North America and around the world.

—PASTOR NEIL CAMPBELL
North American Director,
Family Foundations International

Craig Hill has a unique way of taking biblical truths and breaking them down into a simple language that all can understand. This revelation of the parent's blessing feels like it is straight from God's mouth. It not only will enhance the relationship between a parent and child and exponentially increase the likelihood of a child's success, but it also presents the opportunity to impact our nation for generations to come. Every parent will want to read this book and implement the godly strategy contained in it. When you see in your family the same type of outcome that I have seen with my children, you will want to spread the message contained in this book to all of your friends.

—Ford Taylor
Founder of Transformational Leadership Training,
the FSH Consulting Group,
and cofounder of Transformation Cincinnati

In the early seventies I heard a teaching by a rabbi on imparting blessings to your children. It so moved me that when I had children of my own, my nightly prayers with them included speaking a blessing over their lives. Later on in life when I started doing prison ministry, God impressed on me that because I was a father, I could speak a father's blessing over these men. Speaking a fatherly blessing over these men and watching over half of them break down and cry impacted me deeply. When I read Craig Hill's book, *The Power of a Parent's Blessing*, it was the first time I saw how the Father spoke a blessing over Jesus. As fathers, if we want to influence our children and others, there is not a more powerful way than learning how to bless. I encourage you to read and absorb the deep truths revealed in this book.

—Al Caperna
Chairman of CMC Group and founder of Affirm Global

I have experienced the amazing harm from not having a parent's blessing and the amazing benefits from having that blessing. Just before my unsaved Jewish father died, I asked him to bless me. I believe this blessing not only opened the door for him to be saved, but it also opened the door for God to raise my ministry to a worldwide influence! Most believers have missed the amazing power of the blessing. This book will become a classic and vital piece of your arsenal to fulfill your destiny.

—SID ROTH
Author, host of *It's Supernatural!* television program, and founder of Messianic Vision

THE
POWER
OF A
PARENT'S
BLESSING

THE

POWER

OF A

PARENT'S
BLESSING

CRAIG HILL

CHARISMA
HOUSE

Cover design by Lisa Rae Cox
Design Director: Bill Johnson

Visit the author's website at www.familyfoundations.com.

Library of Congress Cataloging-in-Publication Data:
Hill, Craig S.
  The power of a parent's blessing / Craig Hill.
    pages cm.
  Includes bibliographical references.
  ISBN 978-1-62136-222-7 (trade paper) -- ISBN 978-1-62136-223-4 (ebook)
  1. Parents--Religious life. 2. Child rearing--Religious aspects--Christianity. 3. Benediction. 4. Consecration. I. Title.
  BV4529.H55 2013
  248.8'45--dc22
                              2012049705

People and incidents in this book are composites created by the author from his experiences in ministry. Names and details of the stories have been changed, and any similarity between the names and stories of individuals described in this book to individuals known to readers is purely coincidental.

While the author has made every effort to provide accurate telephone numbers and Internet addresses at the time of publication, neither the publisher nor the author assumes any responsibility for errors or for changes that occur after publication.

First edition

13 14 15 16 17 — 9 8 7 6 5 4 3 2 1
Printed in the United States of America

To my father and mother, Gilman and Vonnie Hill, who understood and used the power of a parent's blessing in my life. I thank God for my parents, who both self-sacrificially poured blessing into my life, empowered me to prosper in my calling, and enabled me to perpetuate a generational cycle of blessing to my wife, children, and grandchildren.

Contents

Introduction

Now the Lord said to Abram, 'Go forth from your country, and from your relatives and from your father's house, to the land which I will show you; and I will make you a great nation, and I will bless you, and make your name great; and so you shall be a blessing; and I will bless those who bless you, and the one who curses you I will curse, and *in you all the families of the earth shall be blessed*'" (Gen. 12:1–3, emphasis added).

God has a plan to bless every family on Planet Earth. That is stated in the promise above, which God made to Abraham the patriarch, foretelling the blessing to come through Jesus Christ, the seed of Abraham. God's stated purpose in sending Jesus the Messiah was to bless all the families of the earth. It is interesting that He did not say He would bless all the individuals of the earth but rather all the families. In this passage in Genesis we see that the primary unit through which God has committed Himself to work is the family. We can also be assured that if God's plan is to bless, then Satan has an opposing plan, and that is to curse all the families of the earth.

So what exactly is blessing and its opposite, cursing? Those terms often bring many different thoughts to mind. Blessing is frequently connected with the receipt of money or some sort of gift. Cursing is oftentimes associated with witchcraft, or someone casting a spell or putting a "curse" on another. Other times we think of cursing as someone using profane or obscene language. While blessing and cursing can certainly mean those things, in this book we are talking about something very simple. Throughout the course of this book we will use the following definitions of these words:

- Blessing: God using a human to impart His message and image of identity and destiny to the heart of another person.

- Cursing: Satan using a human to impart his message and image of identity and destiny to the heart of another person.

God and Satan both have a message they desire to impart into the heart of every person on earth. However, these two messages are totally opposite to each other. While God's message conveys love, value, respect, and purpose, Satan's message conveys shame, a lack of love, and a lack of purpose. At any moment in time parents can be agents of God to bless their children or agents of Satan to curse their children. Parents can impart either God's message—"I love you; you are precious, valuable, and worthy of my time and energy"—or Satan's message—"You are unlovable, unwanted, and not worthy of my time or energy."

In Hebrew, the phrase "to bless" is the word *barak*. The literal translation of this word is "to kneel before someone."[1] So blessing comes from an attitude and posture of humility. When most people think of blessing, they usually think of someone standing over another person and blessing him from a superior position. However, Jesus blessed us by humbling Himself and taking human form. From the posture of a despised criminal, He gave His life to pay for our sin. This is the ultimate image of blessing from a kneeling posture.

While the literal meaning of *barak* is "to kneel before," the primary spiritual connotation is "to empower to prosper."[2] So when you bless someone, you kneel before him in humility and literally empower that person to prosper. Of course, this word *prosper* is not limited to financial prosperity. If you bless your daughter, you empower her to prosper in every area of her life: her spiritual life with God, her physical health, her emotional well-being, her marriage, her children, her finances, her career, and her ministry. To curse is to do the opposite. If you curse your daughter, you likewise cripple, disable, or disempower her from prospering in all of these same areas of life.

In the Greek, the verb "to bless" is the word *eulogeo.* The literal meaning of this word is "to speak well of."[3] This word also means to cause to prosper.[4] Perhaps you have already picked up on its similarity to the English word *eulogy,* which comes from this same root. A eulogy, of course, also means to speak well of, but it is usually given at a funeral. Obviously words spoken at a funeral will not empower the deceased person to prosper. In order to empower someone to prosper, a blessing must be spoken while that person is living and can receive the blessing. So to curse is to speak evil of someone, or to speak Satan's vision or image into someone's life, while to bless is to speak well of someone, or to impart God's vision and image into a person's life.

NUTRIENT-RICH WATER
OR HYDROCHLORIC ACID

One of the best pictures of blessing and cursing came to me one day as I watched my wife, Jan, watering her houseplants. Jan is an expert at growing houseplants. They thrive as she cares for them, and they grow exceedingly large and healthy. When people come to visit us, they often comment on Jan's marvelous green thumb.

When it is time to water the plants, Jan mixes a blue powder containing plant nutrients with water; then she pours just the right amount of the mixture on each plant. I noticed that after each application of this "blue water," the plants seem to perk up and become full of life. Suppose, however, that one day Jan decided to pour hydrochloric acid on her plants instead of the nutrient-enriched water. How might they respond? Instead of thriving, opening up their pores, and craving more, the plants would close all their little pores and attempt to repel as much of the acid as possible.

This example paints a good picture of the power of blessing and cursing. Parents with their words, attitudes, and actions possess the ability to bless or curse the identities of their children. Blessing is like pouring blue, nutrient-rich water over the child's inner being, while cursing is like pouring hydrochloric acid over the child. One empowers the child to prosper; the other cripples and disables. Blessing imparts God's message of identity and destiny while cursing imparts Satan's message of the same.

Even Jesus Needed His Father's Blessing

It is interesting to note that the blessing of a father is so important that Jesus Christ Himself did not perform one miracle or preach one message until after He had publicly received the blessing of God His Father. In the Gospel of Luke we read:

> And the Holy Spirit descended upon Him in bodily form like a dove, and a voice came out of heaven, "You are My beloved Son, in You I am well-pleased."
> —Luke 3:22

Today the phrase the Father spoke over Jesus is not something we typically hear fathers declare to their children. But I am told that the Jews of that time were used to hearing fathers say, "This is my beloved son, in whom I am well pleased." I've been told that it was common for Jewish fathers to speak those words over their sons when releasing them into their adult life and calling. Thus anyone who had ever attended such a

4

Hebrew rite of passage ceremony would have been familiar with the words God the Father declared over Jesus.

The only person over whom this phrase could not be spoken was a person of illegitimate or questionable birth. Because of the strange circumstances of Jesus's birth, many people considered Him illegitimate. Furthermore, because Jesus was not Joseph's biological son, Joseph probably did not pronounce this blessing over Jesus when He was released into adulthood.

In His humanity Jesus may have been tempted to feel insecure about this. Have you ever thought about what it must have been like for Jesus to be God Himself living in human form? At some point in His childhood He must have begun to recognize that He was different from all the other kids. He was entertaining thoughts such as, "I am God. All the fullness of Deity dwells in Me in bodily form."

With whom could He have taken counsel? Who would understand? Can you imagine going to the rabbi and saying, "Excuse me, Rabbi, but I have been thinking some very strange thoughts recently. I actually have been thinking that I am God Himself. What do you think about this?"

Perhaps His mother was the only person who could really understand what life might have been like for Jesus. I believe that in His humanity, Jesus was tempted with the same types of insecurities and fears we face.

Yet if anyone had any doubts about Jesus's identity or destiny, those doubts were absolutely set to rest at the Jordan River when the Father pronounced publicly, "You are My beloved Son. In You I am well pleased." I believe this blessing from His heavenly Father gave Jesus the strength to walk in His true identity and fulfill His destiny on earth. If Jesus needed the blessing of His Father in order to complete His destiny, how much more do our children need to receive a similar blessing from their parents?

Restoring a Culture of Blessing

Unfortunately in our modern Western culture ceremonial blessing at certain critical times in life and weekly parental blessing have been virtually eliminated in most families. When I speak at conferences and in various churches, I often ask the attendees, "How many here were given a blessing ceremony or at least received a powerful impartation of blessing from your father that released you into your adult identity and destiny at or around the time of puberty?"

I asked this very question just recently at a church conference with around two hundred people in attendance. In that group only two individuals raised their hands to say a father had blessed them at the time of puberty.

In many groups I continue my line of questioning by asking, "How many here received a blessing from either your father, mother, or both on a weekly basis?" Again, those who answer affirmatively are even fewer in number than those who received a blessing in some sort of rite of passage ceremony around the time of puberty. Furthermore, those who respond affirmatively generally are not from a traditional Western culture.

The understanding of the power of a parent's blessing has been systematically stolen from our culture. However, in this book you will learn how to restore a culture of blessing to your family and become an ambassador of blessing to your community and those around you.

As I studied the topic of blessing and cursing in the Bible, I identified six critical stages in a child's life when he should receive a blessing from God through his parents, and a seventh time at which children are meant to bless their parents. These seven critical times are: (1) at conception, (2) in the womb, (3) at birth, (4) during infancy, (5) at puberty (in a rite of passage ceremony), (6) at the time of marriage, and (7) in older age.

It would have been virtually impossible for someone growing up in the ancient Hebrew culture to miss out on being blessed at these critical times. The culture was structured in such a way that both ceremonial and day-to-day blessing occurred naturally in most families. This resulted in spiritual, emotional, physical, relational, and financial health for families who practiced the blessing regularly. In the following chapters you will learn how to restore an overall culture of blessing to your own family and how to impart a meaningful blessing to your children every week.

As you read through this book, you will hear the message in two ways: initially as an adult son or daughter, and secondly as a parent to your own children. In each chapter describing the blessing God intended at one of the seven critical times in life, we will look at the power of the blessing and also at the consequences of the lack of blessing or of cursing.

I encourage you to first receive the message for yourself as a son or daughter. Then you will be able to be God's agent to impart to your children the blessing at each critical stage in life.

You may find as you read that you have already missed several of the critical times of blessing in your children's lives. Throughout the book you will learn how you as a parent can still impart the blessing to your older or adult children even if you missed doing so at the appropriate stage in life.

At the end of chapters 4 through 10 you will encounter a section I have called the "Blessing Toolbox." There you will find practical suggestions and prayer models you can use to break the power of curses in your own life and in the lives of your children, as well as prayers you can pray to release the blessing. You also will learn how to close spiritual doors in your family that may have been opened to the enemy and how to open spiritual doors to release God's blessing upon yourself and your children.

You may notice that I use the male pronoun "his" throughout this book when referring to children. This is for ease of reading, not because the blessing pertains only to sons.

If you have daughters, I encourage you to adapt the language as needed.

There is a battle raging within every family over whose message of identity and destiny will be imparted—God's or Satan's. In this book you will learn at exactly what points in your own life and in the lives of your children the enemy has successfully imparted his message and image, and specifically how to replace that image with God's truth. You also will learn how to intentionally bless your family daily, weekly, and at the seven critical times of life. In so doing you will not only empower your own children to prosper, but you will also actually create a legacy of blessing for many generations to come.

You were created to be God's agent of blessing to your children. As you read the following chapters, you will certainly be equipped to empower your own children to fulfill their destinies in God. However, I believe that as you learn to release the power of a parent's blessing, the Lord will also prepare you to be part of a growing army of blessed families who are encouraging others to create a culture of blessing in communities around the world!

Chapter 1

THE CRY OF ESAU

IN GENESIS 27 there is a striking passage containing a message from a son to his father. In verse 34 Esau "cried out with an exceedingly great and bitter cry, and said to his father, 'Bless me, even me also, O my father!'" This cry from the heart of the son, Esau, to his father, Isaac, is the cry of many modern-day adult or adolescent children to their own fathers and mothers.

It is evident that God intended for every child to be blessed by his father and mother at many times in life. Throughout Scripture we see Hebrew parents laying hands on their children and imparting a blessing with words and actions.

In the biblical account of the blessing Isaac was to impart to his sons Jacob and Esau, we see the power and importance of parental blessing. Isaac, his wife, and his sons all understood that a father's blessing upon his firstborn son had tremendous power to cause that son and his family to prosper for generations into the future. This blessing was understood to be so powerful that Jacob, with help from his mother, Rebekah, was willing to lie and cheat in order to obtain the blessing that rightfully belonged to his older brother, Esau.

Pretending to be his brother, Jacob convinced his partially blind father that he was Esau and thereby received from his father the blessing of the firstborn. When Esau subsequently came to his father to receive his blessing and discovered that Jacob had already received their father's irrevocable blessing, Scripture records the following:

> And Esau said to his father, "Have you only one blessing,
> my father? Bless me—me also, O my father!" And Esau
> lifted up his voice and wept…So Esau hated Jacob
> because of the blessing with which his father blessed him,
> and Esau said in his heart, "The days of mourning for my
> father are at hand; then I will kill my brother Jacob."
> —GENESIS 27:38, 41, NKJV

Why did the stolen blessing make Esau so angry that he
wanted to murder his brother? Esau was devastated because he
understood something very few people realize in our modern
times. Esau knew that a father holds a key to his children's
future that, when used, releases them to prosper. When we
follow the life of Jacob through several generations, we observe
that Jacob and his family multiplied in number, became exceedingly wealthy, remained healthy, did not experience plagues
and sickness, conquered their enemies, and ruled in their land
for many generations. The tribe of Esau, on the other hand, did
not prosper, did not become large in number, did not become
wealthy, and was frequently conquered by enemies.

I have observed the same phenomenon in many modern
families. Children whose parents blessed them tend to prosper
in their adult lives, and children whose parents never blessed
them tend to languish. Why is this? I believe it is because God
established the power of blessing and meant it to function in
every family on earth. Blessing is God's primary mechanism
of imparting His image (thoughts, feelings, and experience) of
identity ("Who am I?") and destiny ("Why am I here?") deep
into a person's heart. This is of critical importance because
vision for life, physical and emotional health, financial prosperity, and family relational dynamics are all directly linked
to images of God, self, and others imprinted in the inner man
(soul) of every person (3 John 2).

IDENTITY AND DESTINY

Let's dig a little deeper into identity and destiny and how these concepts relate to blessing and cursing. Whether we realize it or not, every day each one of us answers two critical questions: "Who am I?" and "Why am I here?" We answer these questions based upon preexisting images established deep inside. How we have answered these questions determines the way we respond to life's circumstances.

As I mentioned earlier, the first question—"Who am I?"—pertains to identity. Very simply stated, identity is an individual's perception of himself. The primary issue at stake in dealing with identity is value ("What am I worth?"). So when we speak about identity, we are speaking about a person's perception of himself and the value of his life and being.

The second question—"Why am I here?"—pertains to destiny. This has to do with an individual's perception of his function and significance on earth. The primary issue at stake in dealing with destiny is purpose ("Why am I here? What am I supposed to do?"). Identity and destiny are key qualities that God intended for us to have correctly imparted and established in our lives. The course for our adulthood is set through this impartation of identity and destiny, which we receive as children.

It is and has always been God's intention to impart to each person His message of identity and destiny, especially in particular stages in life. He has appointed special agents on this earth to ensure that His message of identity and destiny is revealed in our hearts. While many people may influence our lives, these special agents of God who are anointed to impart identity and destiny are not angels, teachers, coaches, or pastors. They are *parents*.

If parents do nothing else regarding their children, one task God has given them is to make sure their children receive His message of identity and destiny during their growing-up years.

In contrast, Satan's purpose is to access these agents of God and use them to impart to children his alternate message of identity and destiny.

Imparting God's message of identity and destiny to their children is what I call "blessing." Imparting Satan's alternate message of identity and destiny is what I refer to as "cursing." Many times parents are unwittingly used to impart a spiritual and emotional message from the devil rather than from God.

SATAN'S MESSAGE VS. GOD'S MESSAGE

What is the basic difference between God's message and Satan's? Satan's message of identity goes something like this: "You are nothing, nobody. You have no value. There is something terribly defective and wrong with you. You don't belong here. You're stupid. You're ugly. You're too short (or tall), too fat (or skinny). Your nose is too big. Your skin is the wrong color. You're a mistake. Nobody wanted you to be born. You shouldn't even be here. You're just a product of someone's lust. You're not loved, and no one will ever love you, because you're unlovable." He may also attack a child's gender identity, saying, "You're the wrong sex. Your parents wanted a girl (or a boy). You'll never be accepted, and your parents will always despise you." These are the kinds of messages the devil wants to impart to children early in life.

With regard to destiny ("Why am I here?"), Satan's message sounds something like this: "You shouldn't be here. You don't belong, and you don't fit. You have no purpose, no destiny. You are just consuming oxygen, food, and water on the planet. You are an utterly worthless failure. You are totally incompetent and unproductive. You are completely inadequate in every area of life. Even if you had a destiny from God, you are so defective that even God can't help you complete your destiny. Someone should write a book about your life and call it *The*

Seven Habits of Highly Defective People. You'll never succeed at anything. Nothing will ever work out for you."

God's message of identity and destiny is the opposite. God's answer to the question of identity ("Who am I?") is: "I love you. You mean everything to Me. You are worth the life of My Son, Jesus Christ, because that is what I paid for you. You belong, and you're supposed to be here. You're very special. You are unique. No one else is like you. You're beautiful. I love your hair, your eyes, your skin—everything about you. When I look in your face, you make Me smile. Perhaps your parents weren't expecting you, but I was. You were not a surprise to Me. Your mother carried you for nine months in her womb, but I carried you for thousands of years in My Spirit. And at just the right time I released you to be born on the earth. I knew exactly who you would be and when you would be born. You came right on time. You are the correct sex, exactly who I created you to be. Nothing wrong, nothing defective. You can expect to be loved and valued by others because I love you and created you to be loved."

God's answer to our questions about destiny is much the same. He says, "You belong, and you are here because I created you and uniquely gifted you to be here at this time. You have a unique purpose and destiny that I designed you for, that no one else can fulfill. No one else can be a parent to your children and a child to your own parents. No one else has the unique life experiences, gifts, and skills that you have. You are completely adequate and competent to fulfill your purpose and destiny, but you won't have to do it alone. I have marvelous companions who will accompany you on your journey and help you fulfill your purpose. I Myself will help you and will always be with you. I will never leave you or forsake you. You can expect to prosper and succeed in all I have called you to do in your life. I love you!"

THE EFFECT OF SATAN'S LIES

Many times parents are simply unaware of the power they have as agents of God or of Satan. Not many parents wake up in the morning and say to themselves, "I wonder how I can become Satan's agent today and impart his message to my child on a deep spiritual and emotional level." However, many parents do exactly this without realizing what they have done. That is precisely what happened to Joe.

Joe was a well-dressed, successful businessman in his late thirties when we first met. He and his wife had come to one of the Ancient Paths weekend events our ministry hosts. As we moved into the small-group ministry time, Joe began to share, somewhat sheepishly, how much of a problem anger had become in his life.

"Anger causes me to embarrass myself, and then I feel guilty," Joe explained. He went on to tell us that just a couple of months earlier, he was leaving a shopping mall parking lot and heading into a stream of traffic. Just as he was about to move ahead into the traffic, he realized there really wasn't enough space between the cars for him to enter the traffic flow, so he stopped to wait for a better opening in traffic. Apparently surprised by Joe's sudden decision not to move out in the traffic, the man in the car behind him blew his horn. This is where Joe's story took a rather awkward turn.

"I was so infuriated that he would honk at me, I slammed the gearshift into park and jumped out of my car, almost ripping the door off the hinges on the way," Joe said. "I stormed back to the man's car, grabbed his shirt and jerked his face up through the open window. Then I let him know what I thought of him. The whole time I was screaming at the driver, I was doing all I could to keep from punching him."

When Joe ran out of profanities to spew and thought he had made his point, he returned to his car, and tremendous guilt and shame began to overwhelm him. "I felt almost as if someone else had been shouting those words," Joe said. "'Who was that crazy, raging maniac?' I thought to myself. 'What kind of testimony of the love of Christ did I just present to that man?' Then I remembered the bumper sticker my wife had recently put on both our cars, 'Honk if you love Jesus.' I just sank into a pit of shame and depression all the way home."

Joe said he had gotten so angry with his wife, he was afraid he might physically strike her. When his two-year-old son would wake up crying at night, Joe would have to get out of the house and take a walk; otherwise, he feared he might hurt his young son. "I've prayed and prayed to get rid of this anger," Joe confided. "I've repented of it. I hate it. I've told God that I'll do anything to get rid of it, but nothing seems to work. It's ruining my life and my marriage."

Joe was clearly exasperated, and I felt for him. I suggested to Joe and his wife that we pray and ask the Holy Spirit to reveal the root cause of the anger in his life. Joe agreed, so we began to pray. We simply asked the Lord to show Joe anything that was pertinent to his anger and quietly waited. After a few minutes I asked Joe if the Lord had shown him anything.

"No," he replied, "nothing pertinent."

"What came to your mind?" I pressed.

"Oh, just a dumb experience I had years ago when I was a kid," he said. "As a matter of fact, I had forgotten it until now, but it doesn't have anything to do with my life today."

I urged Joe to share the experience, but he maintained that it wasn't pertinent. Finally I told him, "We asked the Holy Spirit to reveal to you anything that was important, and this experience was the only thing that came to your mind. So why don't we just trust that God was reminding you of that experience for a reason, and perhaps we will discover that it is relevant."

I have found that many times when people have been deeply wounded through the impartation of the devil's message of identity and/or destiny, especially by parents and other influential individuals, the pain is so great that they bury it deep inside and never really deal with it. Because the pain is so intense, they may block key experiences from their memories entirely, and when those memories are brought to the surface, the individuals are completely out of touch with the emotional pain brought on by that event.

As a result, people will oftentimes say things such as "Oh, I've dealt with that," or "I forgave my dad a long time ago for that," or "Oh, that doesn't hurt any more." Christians will even say, "I've put that under the blood of Jesus. He has taken that burden away." However, many times they have not released that pain to the Lord but rather have stuffed it deep inside.

The truth is, there is still a wound that has never been healed but has only been covered over as an oyster covers a grain of sand. The prophet Isaiah described this state when he wrote, "From the sole of the foot even to the head there is nothing sound in it, only bruises, welts and raw wounds, not pressed out or bandaged, nor softened with oil" (Isa. 1:6).

Imagine that you suffered a physical laceration of your arm. Instead of cleaning it out and treating the wound, you never tended to it and simply left it open for all kinds of dirt to get inside. After a while the wound would scab over and might even look as if it were healing, but beneath that outer layer would be a reservoir of infectious puss. In such a situation each time pressure is put on the wound, infectious puss would be released into the body. Eventually, for true healing to come, someone would have to lance the wound, irrigate the infection, cleanse the wound, and close it back up.

This is the picture Isaiah is giving us regarding the inner man. When someone has been deeply wounded spiritually and emotionally, a spiritual cleansing must occur. If it does not, that person might walk around all his life with severe spiritual or emotional "infections" caused by deep wounds that have never been "pressed out or bandaged, nor softened with oil."

Such was the case with Joe. Finally he agreed to share the childhood experience that had come to his mind during prayer, though he continued to maintain that it was not relevant. He said it was so insignificant that he hadn't even remembered it until that moment, and, besides, it didn't hurt any more because he had forgiven his dad years ago.

Joe said that one Friday night when he was eight years old he was allowed to have two friends spend the night with him at his home. He was very excited about this and had been looking forward to the event for some time. Finally the day arrived. The three boys were allowed to stay up later than normal, eat popcorn, and watch scary movies. They were having the time of their lives and finally fell asleep around 1:00 a.m. When Joe awoke the next morning, much to his horror he discovered that something terrible had occurred during the night. He had wet his bed. He did not want his two friends to find out about the accident, so he quickly stripped the bed and hid the sheets and blankets.

However, Joe's mother found the bedding and discovered what had happened. She promptly let Joe's father know. He decided that an appropriate time to discipline Joe would be at the breakfast table in front of his friends and the rest of the family. Not only did Joe's father expose what had happened, but also he then began to ridicule Joe in front of the others. He called him a "bed wetter" and told him they would have to buy him a big diaper to wear. Joe's dad let him know how disappointing it was for him to have an eight-year-old son who still wet the bed. After deriding his son, Joe's father pulled down Joe's pants, bent him over his knee, and gave him a lengthy, bare-bottom spanking right there at the breakfast table in front of his two friends.

After such humiliation, Joe said he just wanted to sink through the floor and disappear. At that moment he wished he could have killed his dad, and if he had a means to do so, he probably would have. "But it doesn't bother me anymore, and I haven't even remembered that experience for over thirty years," Joe told us.

Realizing that Joe probably had some unresolved emotional wounding bottled up inside, I asked if Joe would speak out in prayer to Jesus how he felt while his father was ridiculing and humiliating him in front of his friends that morning many years ago. He agreed to do so. We bowed our heads and closed our eyes to pray, and I waited for Joe to begin speaking to the Lord in prayer. But after about ninety seconds he still had not said anything. I thought that perhaps Joe did not understand that he was to pray aloud, so I invited him again, saying, "Go ahead and just speak out to the Lord how you felt that morning."

Suddenly Joe burst into tears, and thirty years of stored-up hurt, resentment, and anger came flowing out over the next fifteen minutes. He wept and wept and wept as the covered-over wound was finally lanced. I was then able to show Joe how Satan had used his father unwittingly to impart his message of identity and destiny to Joe when he was a small boy. Satan's message was: "You are nothing but a bed-wetter. There is just something inherently wrong with you. No matter how hard you try, you will never succeed at anything in life. You are a shame to your family and an embarrassment to God."

Joe later admitted that this really was how he had felt deep inside all his adult life. He had always believed the deck was stacked against him, and that no matter what he did, circumstances beyond his control always caused him to fail. This would create great frustration and anger that, when acted upon, would further embarrass and shame him.

After releasing all that infectious emotional puss from the inner wound, Joe was then able to forgive his father from his heart and afterward go to God, his heavenly Father, and ask Him to reveal the truth of who Joe really was and why he was here. All Joe's life the Lord had wanted to impart His message of identity and destiny, but the devil's message was already strongly established deep inside. Until that moment Joe could never receive God's opinion of him. As a result, even though Joe was nearly forty years old, in the emotional realm he was still a fearful, insecure eight-year-old boy.

Finally, that day the cork was popped, and all the hurt and anger of the humiliated eight-year-old boy inside Joe was released. For the first time he was able to receive God's message of identity and destiny and be the man God created him to be without feeling like a bed-wetter. Joe's entire life was changed that day. He later said it was like he had lived his entire life in black and white, and that day he discovered a whole new world of color.

It is easy to see how Satan used Joe's father to impart his message of identity and destiny. Joe's dad had no idea the impact that experience would have on his son's life for years to come; he was simply attempting to discipline his son. Joe's dad had no understanding of blessing and cursing or of God's message of identity and destiny versus Satan's. Consequently he unintentionally delivered a message that created an inner image deep in Joe's heart that caused him to spend years of his adult life trying to overcome feelings of worthlessness and failure.

The Bible tells us, "My people are destroyed for lack of knowledge" (Hosea 4:6). Joe's father did not intentionally wound his son; he simply did not know how to send his son God's message rather than Satan's. Without realizing it, Joe's father had cursed his son instead of blessing him.

THE POWER OF A FATHER'S BLESSING

For many people who have never been blessed, the longing for it never goes away. A close friend shared with me a powerful example of how transformative a parent's blessing can be—at any age. My friend Pablo was deeply saddened when his father told him that his mother, who had been living away from home for nine months, was seeking a divorce.

As Pablo pondered what he might do or pray to help his parents, a very strange thought came to him. He had recently experienced a powerful change in the life of his twenty-one-year-old son, José, who had been quite directionless and indecisive. José could not decide if he wanted to enroll in Bible school, university, or get a job. Consequently he was sitting at home doing nothing. Pablo told me that when he looked into his twenty-one-year-old son's eyes, he saw a scared little boy who didn't know what to do and was afraid to make a decision.

About that time Pablo and his wife attended an Ancient Paths Experience and realized the likely reason their son was directionless was that he had never been blessed by his father and released into his adult identity. Consequently, spiritually and emotionally he was still tied to his mother as a little boy.

After attending the Ancient Paths event, Pablo and his wife arranged a blessing ceremony for their son. Pablo told me that immediately after the ceremony, when he looked into his son's eyes, for the first time he saw a confident, twenty-one-year-old man looking back at him rather than a scared little boy. The spiritual and emotional umbilical cord tying José to his mother had literally been cut, and shortly after that, he enrolled in college and began to pursue a career to which he was certain God had called him.

Now upon receiving news of his parents' impending divorce, Pablo had a very strange thought come to mind. Perhaps the deep need in his own father's heart was to be blessed by his father. Pablo remembered looking into his sixty-four-year-old father's eyes and seeing the same scared little boy look he had seen in his twenty-one-year-old son. He suddenly realized that his father, Luis, had never been blessed by his own father and at age sixty-four was still emotionally tied as a little boy to his mother. The reason Luis had struggled in his relationship with his wife was that he had never emotionally left "father and mother" so he could properly "cleave unto his wife" (Gen. 2:24, KJV).

Armed with this understanding, Pablo called his eighty-seven-year-old grandfather, who was still living in the country of their family's origin. Grandpa was quite shocked when Pablo tried to explain his request that on Luis's sixty-fifth birthday he impart his blessing to his son and release him to be a man. Grandpa exclaimed, "You want me to do what? My son is having his sixty-fifth birthday celebration. If he is not a man yet, he never will be." However, Pablo was insistent, and Grandpa finally agreed to come.

Upon Grandpa's arrival, Pablo explained the power of a parent's blessing—a key that he held in his hand as a father to loose his son to prosper. Pablo further explained that Luis was still emotionally bound to his mother as a little boy, with the cry of Esau—"Bless me, even me also, O my father" (Gen. 27:38)—still in his heart at age sixty-five. Grandpa still didn't entirely understand but agreed to attempt to bless his son Luis on his birthday.

When the day of the ceremony arrived, after a time of worship Grandpa and Luis sat opposite each other. Grandpa first attempted to tell his son, "I love you," but got out only the first couple of syllables before he broke into tears. Luis immediately became emotional as well, and all either man could do for the next ten minutes was to sit and weep. When Grandpa tried again to tell his son he loved him, they both broke into tears again. Finally, the third time Grandpa was able to tell his son he loved him and how proud he was of him. He told Luis that he was a huge success because all three of his children loved the Lord and had married godly spouses, and all of Luis's grandchildren were serving Jesus.

Then Grandpa asked, "Son, do you remember when you were fifteen years old?" When his father asked this question,

Luis suddenly began to release a huge surge of emotional pain. Yes, Luis remembered when he was fifteen years old. What no one else knew was that Luis and his father had a huge argument that became physical. That day Luis's father had screamed horrible things at his son. He told Luis that he was worthless and physically threw him out of the house. He told him he hated him and hoped he would never see this worthless son again.

Luis, of course, had become equally angry and said horrible things to his father also. He told his father that he hated him as well and would never see him again. He left the house in rebellion at age fifteen to begin his adult life. Obviously this was not the blessing Luis needed to be released into his adult identity.

Luis and his father had since reconciled, but in fifty years they had never spoken of the event. When Luis's father brought it up, his words stirred up fifty years of bitterness, hatred, resentment, and anger that had been in Luis's heart. Years ago he had said he forgave his father, but his heart had never released the pain, and he had neither truly forgiven his father nor repented of the bitterness, dishonor, and rebellion that had been in his heart toward his dad.

Now fifty years later, when his father lanced the infectious wound, Luis burst into profuse sobbing. Luis buried his face in his father's chest as his father also sobbed profusely. When Grandpa's sobs had subsided enough for him to speak, he whispered to Luis, "Son, I'm so sorry. I was wrong that day. Please forgive me. I got angry, said things I didn't mean, and cursed you instead of blessed you. Please forgive me. I love you!" Those words only intensified his son's sobbing.

When Luis finally stopped weeping, his dad looked into his eyes and said, "Son, I love you. I was wrong. Will you forgive me for the words I said and the way I treated you growing up in general and specifically on the day you left home?" Luis replied, "Yes, Papa, I forgive you. I love you. I also was wrong in my attitude and the words I spoke. Will you forgive me?"

Grandpa responded, "Yes, of course. I love you, son. And today I pronounce over you the words I should have spoken fifty years ago. Son, I'm proud of you. You are not a foolish little boy. You are a man. Today I bless you. I cut you loose emotionally and spiritually from your mother, and I give you my blessing and release you into your adult identity as a man. Go and be and do all God has called you to."

As Pablo shared this story with me, he related that something supernatural had happened in the heart of his father, Luis, the day he received his father's blessing. Pablo said after the blessing ceremony, when he looked into his father's eyes, he saw a bold, confident sixty-five-year-old man who was at peace. No longer was Luis that frightened little boy, and it showed.

The supernatural healing that took place in Luis's heart that day was so profound that two weeks later Pablo's mother cancelled her plans for divorce and moved back home. She said, "I don't know what happened to my husband, but finally I got the man I thought I married. For the last forty-five years I have been trying to follow an angry little boy who didn't know where he was going and who frequently blamed me for his own failures and frustrations. Somehow the fear, anger, frustration, and blame are now all gone. This is the man I fell in love with forty-five years ago. I don't want to divorce him. I love him and want to live the rest of my life with him."

Luis and his wife spent the next several months sharing a new honeymoon. They spent many more years prospering in business and devoting much of their time to helping other couples in their city. Luis later told Pablo, "I had no idea that my heart had been longing for the blessing of my father for over fifty years. I knew it would be good to see my father, but I had no idea that his blessing would be such a key to change my image and experience of myself and of life."

Pablo also spoke to his grandpa after the blessing ceremony. Grandpa told him, "If I had known that my blessing as a father was the key that would unlock future prosperity for my son, I would have used it many decades ago. I only regret that I made this discovery so late in my son's life and that it took my grandson to motivate me to do what I should have done decades ago."

We see in this story the power of a parent's blessing. Without realizing it, Luis had been waiting all his adult life to receive his father's blessing. Not having this blessing had negatively impacted his marriage as well as his sense of personal value and purpose. The two primary reasons Luis's father never blessed him are the same reasons many of us don't bless our sons and daughters. The first reason is lack of knowledge. No one ever taught us the power of a parent's blessing to either release our children into future prosperity or hinder it.

The second is lack of experience. It is very difficult to give something we have never received. If our own parents did not know about or experience blessing while they were growing up, they were neither able to bless us at critical times in life nor rear us in a culture and lifestyle of blessing. As a consequence, it is very difficult for many of us who are now parents to impart blessing to our children. Like Luis, we as adult children are crying out as Esau did, "Bless me, even me also, O my father." You can change this pattern and leave a new legacy for future generations by creating a family culture of blessing.

Chapter 2

CREATING A FAMILY
CULTURE OF BLESSING

I BELIEVE IT IS God's plan for every child to do more than receive his parents' blessing once in his life. God wants children to grow up in a culture of blessing. You may be wondering what exactly a culture of blessing is. This is simply an environment in which family members regularly convey to one another God's message of value rather than Satan's message of worthlessness. In a culture of blessing, family members regularly pour the blue plant fertilizer rather than the hydrochloric acid over one another's lives. They desire to see one another prosper.

No one will be able to do this 100 percent of the time. However, in a family that blesses, when someone inadvertently or even intentionally curses the identity of another family member, as soon as the offense is recognized, that person repents and makes things right. In a culture of blessing, family members hold one another accountable to be God's agents of blessing.

Many people groups around the world practice customs, ceremonies, and traditions that naturally produce an overall culture of blessing. God gave the Jewish people a wonderful tradition of weekly family blessing that is practiced even to this day. I am speaking of the tradition of gathering the family together each week on Friday evening (*Erev Shabbat* in Hebrew) for a special meal and a pronouncement of blessing. (With the busy schedules of most modern families, getting everyone together for a meal would be a miracle in and of itself.)

Each week at this time the Jewish father prays a blessing over his wife. He then pronounces a blessing over each of his children. In many Jewish families the father also proclaims vision and prosperity over his children, thus creating in his offspring an expectation of future success. By so doing, such a father, whether he knows it or not, is imparting God's image of identity and destiny into the hearts and minds of his children. In many Jewish families who practice this tradition, the words of blessing the father speaks over his children are prophetic, and in adulthood the children fulfill exactly what the father prophesied week after week.

Why would the Jewish young person think, "I should own the bank," while the Christian young person thinks, "I should work at the bank"? I believe that many times this is because of a vision that was imparted week after week through parental blessing. While the Christian young person thinks, "I hope to get a job at the movie studio," the Jewish young person thinks, "I should own the movie studio," or "I should be the foremost film director of all time." This is the power of vision imparted through a parent's blessing.

I also have observed that in some Christian families, because there is no tradition of regular blessing, the children primarily hear words of correction and criticism from their parents. Sometimes those words inadvertently impart Satan's vision and image rather than God's. Most parents are blind to the power their words and actions have to bless or curse their children.

For example, a father may say to his fifteen-year-old daughter, "You're not going out of the house in those clothes. That top is cut way too low, and those jeans are too tight. You're showing too much skin. You look like a prostitute! If you keep dressing like that and hanging around with your current friends, you'll probably end up pregnant within a year."

Those kinds of words can prove to be prophetic, and the children fulfill exactly what their parents have spoken over them. I really don't think God intended Jewish families to have a monopoly on the weekly blessing of their children. Every one of us could implement this tradition into our own families. If you would like to see an example of a father blessing his son, visit my YouTube channel at CraigHill3 and click on the video "Speak Blessing Over Your Children."

CONTROL VS. AUTHORITY

While it is important to have specific, regular times of blessing, such as at a weekly meal, it is equally important for parents to establish a general atmosphere of blessing rather than cursing in their home. In order to do this, parents must learn how to separate their children's identity from their behavior. This is particularly important when the need to discipline arises.

I remember one of the first times the Lord showed me that I was about to curse my son rather than bless him when I needed to administer discipline. My youngest son, Jonathan, was four years old, and I was in my first year of being a pastor. After a wonderful church service I walked out into the foyer, and there was Jonathan's Sunday school teacher standing there with Jonathan.

She greeted me and said, "Pastor, we had a little problem with Jonathan in the class this morning. I asked him to do something, and he told me no. I asked again, and he told me no again, but then called me a very obscene name. We took care of the problem in the class, but I thought you as his father would want to know."

I felt my face turning three shades of red. I was thinking, "How could he do this to me? The teacher probably thinks this is how we speak in our home." Then I immediately thought of 1 Timothy 3:5, a scripture regarding the requirements for Christian elders and ministers. It says, "If a man does not know how to manage his own household, how will he take care of the church of God?" I thought, "My ministry is over! My son is out of control, and I have to resign."

I felt a huge rush of shame and embarrassment, which was soon followed by anger. I thought, "I'll spank Jonathan right here, right now, and show this teacher I am a good father and that I think this is very serious." But as I moved toward Jonathan, the Holy Spirit stopped me and asked, "What are you doing?"

"I'm disciplining my son," I said.

"No, you're not. You are about to become Satan's agent and curse his identity."

"What?" I replied, "No, Jonathan did something wrong, and he needs discipline. And as his father, I am the appointed and anointed agent to administer that discipline."

The Lord then said to me, "That is true, but at this particular moment you are disqualified."

"Disqualified? Why?" I argued.

The Lord then reminded me of Matthew 7:3, which says in essence, before you try to remove the speck from your brother's eye, remove the beam from your own eye. The Lord then said to me, "You have such a large beam in your own eye, you can't see clearly to remove the speck from your son's eye. You don't want to discipline him for his benefit. Your heart is filled with anger, and you want to discipline him to justify yourself in the eyes of the teacher and to vent your wrath on him for embarrassing you."

The Lord went on to say to me, "Because you feel like a failure as a father, you are going to take all your frustration out on your little son and through your anger make him feel worse than you do. You are about to impart to your son the devil's message. Satan's anti-gospel message connects value to performance, while My gospel disconnects value from performance.

"Satan's anti-gospel says, 'If you obey and do right, I'll love, value, and bless you. But if you disobey and do wrong, I'll withhold love, take your value, and curse you.' You were about to curse your son's identity because he used an obscene word and embarrassed you."

The Lord continued, "My gospel says this, 'If you obey and do right, I'll love, value, and bless you. However, if you disobey and do wrong, I'll still love, value, and bless you. But I will also discipline your behavior with a consequence appropriate to your wrong choice. Yet My love and value for you never changes no matter what you do.' This is the message I want you to convey to your son."

This was a shocking revelation to me, and I didn't understand what was happening in my heart. I asked the Lord, "Why am I so embarrassed and angry at Jonathan?"

I immediately heard Him say, "Son, this is because you still don't really believe that I love you and that your value in My sight is not dependent upon your performance. You have to do everything perfectly in order to feel valuable, and now you have extended that same lie to your son. If he sins or makes a mistake, then you feel like a worthless father and blame him for discrediting you. So in reality your emotional well-being is now dependent upon the behavior of a four-year-old boy.

"Responsibility for the emotional well-being of another person would be a pretty heavy burden to place on an adult, but to make a four-year-old responsible for your emotional state is totally unfair to him. If he behaves properly, you feel valuable and OK emotionally. But if he misbehaves, you feel worthless and angry, so you blame him for those feelings, curse his identity, and make him feel more worthless than you do. In so doing, you become an agent spreading Satan's anti-gospel to your son."

What a revelation! Instead of proceeding with my original plan, I told Jonathan that I would talk to him when we got home. After spending an hour with the Lord to get at the root of my own shame and inability to feel valuable when my son had sinned, I finally was able to tell Jonathan that I loved him and that even though he had done wrong, he was still just as valuable to me and my love for him had not changed. I then was able to discipline him without anger for being disrespectful to his teacher. I was able to use a respectful tone of voice and bless his spirit even while I disciplined him. As far as I know, he was never disrespectful to his teacher like that again.

When identity and behavior are fused in a parent's mind, that parent will think blessing the identity of a child when he misbehaves is the same as condoning the child's behavior. Consequently, in an attempt to discipline his son's or daughter's behavior, the parent will curse the child's identity. Is it right to bless a rebellious, misbehaving child? Certainly! Blessing should be predicated upon who the child is, not what he does.

Many times the primary root of teenage rebellion is lack of parental blessing. *God meant for us to bless the person and discipline the behavior.*

I'm grateful that God is able to separate our behavior from our identity and doesn't base His love for us on what we do. The Bible tells us, "God demonstrates His own love toward us, in that while we were yet sinners, Christ died for us" (Rom. 5:8).

I cannot think of a greater blessing and confirmation of love than to die for another person. The fact that Jesus died for you and conveyed His acceptance of you while you were still rebelling against Him does not mean He also approved of your sinful behavior. He separated who you are (identity) from what you do (behavior). In this way God can bless who you are but not necessarily condone what you do.

When parents fail to separate identity from behavior, they

fall into the trap of either condoning wrong behavior in an attempt to bless the child or cursing the child's identity in an attempt to administer discipline. When this happens, a parent will tend to lead his family according to the devil's system of governance rather than God's. Satan uses a governance system based on control. God, on the other hand, governs through the exercise of authority. Let me define these terms as I will use them here.

1. Control entails using the manipulative power of the soul to force (threaten or intimidate) others to do your will.

2. The exercise of authority entails honoring the personhood and will of others by offering them choices that bring consequences.

While control does not honor or often even acknowledge the free will of others, the exercise of authority consistently honors people's choices while also consistently applying consequences for wrong choices. God has always honored people's choices. He has never forced anyone to receive Jesus Christ. He offers choices with consequences. For example, He may offer you the choice to: (a) receive Jesus Christ and live in His presence for all eternity, or (b) reject Jesus Christ and live separated from Him in hell for all eternity. He implores you to select choice A, as it will be much better for you, but the decision is yours.

In Deuteronomy 30:19 God said, "I call heaven and earth to witness against you today, *that I have set before you life and death, the blessing and the curse.* So choose life in order that you may live, you and your descendants" (emphasis added). Again we see God offering choices with consequences. I believe His intention is for us to govern our children the same way He governs us. Unfortunately, in their experiences growing up, most parents have known only the system of control. Their parents controlled them, and they use the same methods with their children. They likely don't realize that Satan's system of control breeds an environment of cursing. God's system of authority, on the other hand, nurtures an environment of blessing.

For many parents the most difficult time to walk out a culture of blessing is when their children are disobedient or rebellious. It is easy to bless those who are doing what you want them to do. It is harder to bless a child who is resistant to parental authority, stubborn, and rebellious. As a result, many parents end up cursing the identity of their children during times of discipline without even realizing it.

THREE CRITICAL COMPONENTS OF DISCIPLINE

Many years ago I learned that in order to create a culture of blessing and separate identity from behavior in dealing with my children, I would have to learn to implement the three components of family governance conveyed in Proverbs 6:23. This scripture tells us, "For the commandment is a lamp and the teaching is light; and reproofs for discipline are the way of life." So we see that the three components of discipline are:

1. A commandment

2. A teaching

3. A reproof

The first component—the commandment—is to ensure I have clearly conveyed to my child what is expected of him. If I discipline my child for something I never told him he was supposed to do, it will wound his heart and create confusion. So the first step is to clearly state what is required of the child.

Second comes the teaching. It is important to explain to the child in age-appropriate language why this rule is important. If you give a child a command without explaining why it exists, that child will learn to obey only when you are around to apply a consequence. Yet if a child learns the wisdom behind the command, he can chose to obey that command not because he fears punishment but because he understands the purpose for the restriction.

The third component is reproof. This is the application of a consequence when a command is violated. Remember, God governs by offering choices with consequences. The reproof is that consequence. If a parent never establishes or applies a consequence for violating a command, he makes the rule of none effect in his children's lives and teaches them that the parent's command means nothing.

Many parents fail to separate identity from behavior and bless their children when they discipline (thus disciplining their children in anger) for three simple and practical reasons. Some never learned God's system of governance. Others understand the system but fail to determine in advance which decisions to leave to the child's discretion and which ones require boundaries with enforceable consequences. Still other parents set boundaries and teach their children the purpose for the commands but then wrongly assume their offspring will naturally obey.

Unfortunately it is human nature to test given boundaries. So if parents don't plan in advance where to set boundaries and which consequences to apply when—not if—their children test the boundaries and violate the command, they are left scrambling trying to decide what to do.

When parents haven't thought through what consequence to apply when a child violates a boundary, it is very easy for them to slip into Satan's governing method by cursing the child's identity in an attempt to control his behavior. This then results in heated emotional exchanges, especially with teenagers, and serves to create an environment of cursing rather than blessing. This has led to great emotional damage in many families, with both the parents and the children basically attempting to tolerate one another. In more severe situations this wounding leads to a deep dislike or hatred. Let me give you an example.

TAKE OUT THE TRASH

Emily was a frustrated mother who could never seem to get her seventeen-year-old daughter to do her chores. Emily's daughter, Cathy, was responsible to collect the trash on Tuesday nights and set it outside for pickup early Wednesday morning. Yet week after week Tuesday night would roll around, and Cathy would be in her room in her pajamas, texting her friends or chatting with them on Facebook, and the trash would not be on the curb.

Emily would remind her daughter of her responsibility, and Cathy would promise to take it out in the morning before school, but Emily would insist she take it out right then. "No," Emily would say. "You have said you'd take it out in the morning, but then we missed the trash pickup because you didn't get up early enough. Then we are stuck with bags of stinky trash for another week. Please get up and take the trash out now."

Cathy would again promise to do her chores before school the next day. "No, Mom," she'd say. "I'll set my alarm and get up to take it out in the morning. I promise."

Emily would get agitated, knowing her daughter rarely took the trash out in the morning, and Cathy would whine about already being in her pajamas. "Don't 'But Mom' me!" Emily would say, her tone rising in intensity. "I want you to get up and do it now."

Emily would continue to insist, and Cathy would continue to dig in her heels: "Mom, you're a trash Nazi! You treat everybody like you're Hitler running a prison camp. There's no reason I can't do this in the morning. Why does everything have to be done exactly your way?"

This exchange would go on for some time, with Emily getting more and more agitated until she was screaming and taking the gadgets away from Cathy so she'd get up and take out the trash. Cathy would rush off in tears, shouting that she hated her mother. Then Emily would give up, telling Cathy the trash had better be ready for pickup in the morning. Of course Cathy would oversleep, and the trash would be left uncollected.

At that point Emily would completely lose her temper and begin shouting at Cathy, calling her a worthless, lazy, irresponsible pain in the rear. Cathy would then rush out the door, yelling insults back at her mom. This cycle repeated itself week after week.

Without realizing it, Emily had become Satan's agent rather than God's in her daughter's life. She had created a culture of cursing in her home rather than blessing. Emily was at a total loss as to what else to do because no one had ever taught her God's system of authority.

Fortunately Emily attended one of our Blessing Generations Experiences, which was held at her church. That weekend Emily was deeply convicted that she had been used as Satan's agent to curse her daughter rather than to bless her. Emily wept bitterly before the Lord as she remembered all the times she had attacked Cathy's identity and conveyed Satan's message of worthlessness to her daughter. She simply didn't know how to deal with Cathy's strong will.

When Emily returned home Saturday evening, she asked Cathy if she could talk with her. After finishing a text, Cathy joined her mom at the kitchen table.

"Cathy," Emily began with tears in her eyes, "I just realized this weekend that I have treated you like a Nazi prison camp commander instead of like a mother. In an attempt to get you to do what I wanted, I have threatened you, forced you, coerced and yelled at you, and treated you with great disrespect and dishonor. I never saw this as wrong or as sin against you until this weekend. I didn't know any other way to try to correct you. Could you please find it in your heart to forgive me? I really want to change and be to you the mother God wants me to be."

Cathy began to tear up, never expecting to hear her mother say such things. After getting over her shock, Cathy replied, "Yes, Mom. I do forgive you. I never thought I would hear these words from you. All my life you have treated me like nothing I ever do or say is right in your sight. This is the first time I've heard you acknowledge that anything you did was wrong."

During the Blessing Generations Experience Emily realized that she had learned from her mother to never acknowledge a mistake or admit to any wrongdoing. "Cathy," Emily said, "I now know that what you're saying is true. My mother was exactly like that with me. I thought that since I was your mother, it was my job to force you to obey me. I never realized until yesterday that this is how Satan treats people, not how God treats His children. I have been so wrong in how I've treated you. Please forgive me."

"I do forgive you, Mom," Cathy said. "And I know that I have also said hurtful and disrespectful things back to you. Would you please forgive me too?"

Emily, weeping openly now, got up from her chair and embraced her daughter. "Of course I will," she said. "I'm so sorry for the way I've treated you. I love you! You are a wonderful young woman of God with incredible potential. You're smart, you're beautiful, and God has gifted you to be a leader. I notice that others follow you into whatever you get into. I'm so proud of you as my daughter, and I love you very much."

Mother and daughter embraced for a while longer before Emily returned to her chair. She then told Emily, "I'd like to take some time tomorrow to talk with you about how your dad and I would like to correct your behavior in the future."

"Sure, Mom," said Cathy.

The following day Emily and her husband, Kurt, explained to their daughter what they had learned over the weekend about governing with God's system of the exercise of authority instead of Satan's system of control. "I have never acknowledged or honored your will," Emily told Cathy. "I have treated you as if there is only one will here: *my will.* I now realize that is wrong. From now on we will offer you choices with consequences rather than trying to coerce and force you to do our will."

"For example," Kurt added, "regarding your chore of taking out the trash on Tuesday evenings, we are both so sorry for the way we have treated you in the past. Would you please forgive us?"

"Yes," Cathy said.

"From now on we will offer you a choice with a consequence. So, you do agree that it is your responsibility to collect and take out the trash by the time you leave for school Wednesday morning?"

"Yes," Cathy said. "And I'll try to do better to really get it done on time."

"Great," Kurt replied. "In any case, neither your mom nor I will harass you about it. How and when you do it is your choice. However, there will be consequences to your choices. You may choose to make sure the trash gets out by the time you leave on Wednesday morning. The consequence of that choice is that we will all live trash-free for the next week. Or you could choose to not get the trash out by the time you leave. The consequence of that choice is that you will have to take personal responsibility for the trash that was not removed. Do you understand?"

Cathy did not fully understand what her father was telling her, but she liked her parents' new attitude and was glad her mom promised not to yell at her about the trash anymore. So she said, "Sure, Dad, that's fine."

"One last thing," Emily added. "We highly recommend that you take out the trash on time. I think it will be much more pleasant for you, and you will enjoy it more."

Cathy replied, "OK, Mom."

The next Tuesday evening Cathy chose to collect and take out the trash before she got ready for bed. Emily was pleased and thought their talk had done some good. However, the next week Emily found Cathy in her pajamas and on her iPad late Tuesday evening, and the trash had not been collected or taken out. This time Emily was at peace, as she realized that it was not her responsibility to "control" Cathy. She had given Cathy clear choices. Instead of yelling at her daughter, Emily went into Cathy's room and kissed her good night. All she said was, "Remember, sweetie, tomorrow is trash day."

Cathy's reply was, "I know, Mom. I'll do it in the morning."

Emily said good night and went on about her evening. The next morning, of course, Cathy got up late. She had no time to deal with the trash; she just grabbed a piece of toast and ran out of the house at the last moment to get to school. Emily was completely at peace, as again she realized that it was not her job to control Cathy. It was her job to give the command— the instruction—and apply the consequence. God was the only one who could change Cathy.

When Cathy got home from school that afternoon, she greeted her mom on the way to her room. She was feeling a bit guilty because she knew she had not taken out the trash that morning. Cathy was sort of expecting her mom to yell at her about it, but Emily was pleasant. She didn't say a thing about the trash; she just asked Cathy about her day at school. Cathy was a little shocked by her mom's calm demeanor. "Maybe she really has changed," Cathy thought.

After the brief exchange with her mom Cathy went upstairs

to her room. Then about twenty seconds later she came running back down with a horrified look on her face. "Mom, there are five bags of trash sitting on the floor in my room!" she exclaimed.

"I know," Emily said calmly. "Remember the conversation we had about choices and consequences?"

"Yes," Cathy said, "but why are there five bags of trash in the middle of my floor?"

"Well, as you remember, we explained that there would be a consequence to each choice. You chose to not take out the trash on time. We explained to you that if you made that choice, you would have to take personal responsibility for the trash. Since you chose not to take the trash out in time for it to be taken away, it is only fair that you keep the trash in your space until next week. None of the rest of us are responsible for the trash or want it in our space."

"But Mom!" Cathy cried. "It stinks, and it takes up half my room."

"I'm so sorry, honey," Emily said. "I know it is not pleasant. This is why we highly recommended that you take out the trash. We thought you would enjoy the consequence more. But you chose the other option. That means until next Tuesday evening you'll have to keep the trash in your room. I want you to know, sweetheart, that we're not doing this because we're angry with you. We love you very much. You're our daughter. You're beautiful, you're smart, and God has an incredible destiny for your life. But you made your choice, and this is the consequence. God bless you, sweetie. Have a good night."

That was the last time Cathy failed to take the trash out before she left for school on Wednesday mornings. Kurt and Emily learned how to offer choices that have clear consequences, but to let Cathy choose rather than try to control and manipulate her by yelling and threatening her. When they used God's system of governance, they had to apply the consequence for the wrong choice only once. Had they continued to use Satan's system, they would have had to nag Cathy almost every week to get her to take out the trash.

This was the first of many experiences that helped rebuild a healthy relationship between Cathy and her parents. Exercising authority that honors a person's free will while applying consequences for wrong choices can totally change the atmosphere in your home, even if you never before experienced this kind of parenting yourself. God's system of governance works!

How to Establish a Time of Family Blessing

Without a structured, regular time of blessing, children likely hear only words of correction and discipline from their parents. Why not create a tradition of weekly blessing for your family? The key to making this work practically is to follow the model Jewish families established and prioritize this time of blessing above all other activities you or your children may be involved in. You can start your own tradition in your home by following these three steps.

1. *Have a meal together.*

2. *After the meal initiate a time of repentance and blessing.* Because no one can receive blessing when he is carrying an emotional wound from the one seeking to bless, I suggest you begin your blessing time by addressing offenses, perceived or real. I have found that if you look directly into your child's eyes you will immediately be able to discern if there is an offense or unhealed emotional wound. An offended person will have a hard time maintaining eye contact with someone who has offended him.

If you discern an offense or emotional distance between you and your child, I suggest starting your time of blessing with repentance. If you know you have emotionally wounded or cursed the identity of one of your children during the week, acknowledge the offense and ask forgiveness. Even if you were not entirely in the wrong, if there is an offense or wound in your child's heart and you sense emotional distance between you, seek to repair this by acknowledging the offense and repenting for causing hurt. Commit to bridge any emotional distance between you.

3. *Bless each family member.* When all the wounds and offenses are dealt with, you can then bless each child individually. I suggest that you use the five key components of blessing outlined by John Trent and Gary Smalley in their landmark book on the topic, *The Blessing.* These components of a blessing are:

- Appropriate meaningful touch
- A spoken word
- Attaching high value to the one being blessed
- Picturing a special future for the one being blessed
- An active commitment to help fulfill the blessing[1]

You may have seen the movie *Fiddler on the Roof.* The Sabbath prayer Tevye and Golda speak over their daughters is a good example of the type of blessing you may consider declaring over your children.

May the Lord protect and defend you.
May He always shield you from shame.
May you come to be
In Israel a shining name.

May you be like Ruth and like Esther.
May you be deserving of praise.
Strengthen them, O Lord,
And keep them from the strangers' ways.

May God bless you and grant you long lives.
May the Lord fulfill our Sabbath prayer for you.
May God make you good mothers and wives.
May He send you husbands who will care for you.

May the Lord protect and defend you.
May the Lord preserve you from pain.
Favor them, Oh Lord, with happiness and peace.
Oh, hear our Sabbath prayer. Amen.[2]

The family blessing extends beyond your children. If you are married, make it a daily practice to pray blessing over your spouse. You don't have to spend a lot of time doing this; just a few minutes a day will do. Find a consistent time that works for you as a couple. When you bless each other, be sure to face your spouse and pray with your eyes open. You need to look into your spouse's eyes so you can convey blessing not only with your words but also with your eyes and facial expression. You can spend a minute or two doing each of the following:

1. Repenting if God shows you that you have wounded or sinned against your spouse in the previous twenty-four hours

2. Thanking God for your spouse (acknowledging the qualities you appreciate about her/him)

3. Pronouncing blessing over your spouse and her/ his day

Establishing a tradition of blessing will transform your relationships with your spouse and your children. You are speaking life into their present and their future and expressing the deep love you have for them. By setting aside time each week for a time of family blessing, you are also teaching by example that your family is a priority above all other obligations. If you make this kind of investment into your family, it will bear fruit for generations to come.

Chapter 3

GOD'S ANCIENT PATH:
SEVEN CRITICAL TIMES OF BLESSING

IMPARTING BLESSING AS a lifestyle and at seven critical stages of life sets the foundation of identity and destiny that will empower generations to prosper. Although this lifestyle of blessing is found in the Bible and is expressed through the Jewish culture, this is not just a Jewish way to live. God established these principles of blessing for every family. A lifestyle of blessing is one of God's "ancient paths," a term taken from the Book of Jeremiah.

> Thus says the LORD, "Stand by the ways and see and *ask for the ancient paths*, where the good way is, and walk in it; and *you will find rest for your souls*. But they said, 'We will not walk in it.'"
> —JEREMIAH 6:16, EMPHASIS ADDED

This scripture caught my attention many years ago as I realized that much of the family dysfunction in our day— the addictions, abuse, adultery, and abandonment—stemmed directly from the fact that many parents lacked rest in their souls. When a person lacks a deep, settled sense of intrinsic value (identity) and purpose (destiny), that individual's soul will not be at rest. Instead it will continually search for love, significance, and purpose. As I have said earlier, blessing is God's mechanism within families to bring a child's soul into rest and impart a secure sense of value and purpose.

A parent who has never received a parent's blessing himself is continually searching for blessing and therefore cannot focus on imparting blessing to the next generation. In this passage in Jeremiah the prophet tells us that if we will ask for, embrace, and walk in God's ancient paths, we will naturally find rest for our souls. Children who grow up in this kind of family environment will naturally experience rest in their souls.

In subsequent chapters, as we look in detail at each of the seven critical times of blessing, we will find that God placed in the ancient Hebrew culture ceremonies, traditions, laws, and common societal attitudes that would make it very difficult for a person to not be blessed in all seven critical stages. In that culture, blessing at these times was a normal occurrence in every family. A parent would have had to deviate from the norm to avoid blessing his children.

Unfortunately today none of the cultural safeguards God established to ensure blessing at these critical stages are still intact. Even a Christian parent would have to deviate significantly from the cultural norm to ensure his children were blessed at the seven critical stages in life.

WHY DO JEWISH PEOPLE PROSPER?

As I have traveled to many nations, I have found that Jewish people everywhere tend to prosper financially, educationally, and in their family relationships more than almost any other culture in the world. It doesn't matter whether you're in New York, Paris, Tel Aviv, Sao Paulo, Sydney, or Hong Kong—Jewish families tend to prosper above others in the culture. In the back of my mind I have often wondered why this is. I also wondered if this was just my perception or if there truly was substance to the impression I had.

Then recently I came across a book called *The Jewish Phenomenon* by Steven Silbiger.[1] This book confirmed what I had suspected. Silbiger begins by saying his book "takes a positive position, that the Jewish people have been successful because of a combination of factors related to the Jewish religion and culture and a collective historical experience." He then says there are things *"everyone and any group can examine and learn from"* (emphasis added).[2]

Silbiger, who is Jewish, said his parents expected him to achieve economically and educationally, and he had numerous role models in his family, his community, the media, and cities around the world to reinforce that idea. Economic success was the norm in the Jewish community he grew up in. He writes:

> Did I buy into a stereotype perpetuated out of ethnic pride, or was there a truth to it? Being critical by nature, I quickly uncovered some compelling facts that prove Jewish success is indeed a fact in America:
>
> - The percentage of Jewish households with income greater than $50,000 is double that of non-Jews.
>
> - On the other hand, the percentage of Jewish households with income less than $20,000 is half that of non-Jews.
>
> - "The Jewish advantage in economic status persists to the present day; it remains higher than that of white Protestants and Catholics, even among households of similar age, composition and location."
>
> - Forty percent of the top 40 of the Forbes 400 richest Americans are Jewish.
>
> - "One-third of American multimillionaires are tallied as Jewish."
>
> - Twenty percent of professors at leading universities are Jewish.
>
> - Forty percent of partners in the leading law firms in New York and Washington are Jewish.

- Thirty percent of American Nobel Prize winners in science and 25 percent of all American Nobel winners are Jewish.[3]

How could such a small percentage of the American population—only 2 percent—account for such a large percentage of the educated, wealthy, and influential people in our society? Why would Christians, whom the Bible tells us in Romans 11 are grafted into covenant with the God of Abraham, Isaac, and Jacob by the blood of Jesus Christ, not manifest at least the same or even better statistics than the Jewish people? This was baffling to me until the Lord gave me a deeper understanding of 3 John 2: "Beloved, I pray that in all respects you may prosper and be in good health, *just as your soul prospers*" (emphasis added).

As I read this verse, I saw the key reason Jewish people prosper in their natural lives in ways many Christians do not. They follow customs and traditions (ancient paths) established by God that have caused the souls of their children to prosper. Many Christians are alive in their spirit and have spiritual traditions that cause the spirits of their children to prosper. However, according to the verse in 3 John, prosperity in life and health is dependent upon prosperity in the soul (mind, will, and emotions).

While Christian families *may* create a culture that causes the spirits of their children to prosper, Jewish families *tend* to create a culture that causes the souls of their children to prosper. So as new covenant believers, why don't we learn how to create a family culture that prospers both the spirit and the soul of our children?

You may ask, "So what types of customs and traditions do Jewish people practice that tend to cause their souls to prosper?" I believe the answer lies in the custom we discussed in the previous chapter: the parent's blessing. As we have already seen, all parents are prophets to their children, but not all prophecies are from God. I believe the souls of Jewish children tend to prosper not only because of the weekly Sabbath blessing of their parents but also because their culture naturally facilitates the blessing of children at several of the seven critical stages of life.

Although the concept of blessing is clearly expressed in biblical Hebrew culture and we see remnants of it in modern Jewish culture, I don't believe God intended for Jewish people to have a monopoly on blessing. I believe God intended for the lifestyle of blessing and the impartation of blessing at the seven critical times of life to function naturally in every family and culture on earth. These traditions of blessing did not originate with Jewish people but are ancient paths originating from God and intended for everyone everywhere.

BLESSING IN EIGHTEENTH-CENTURY AMERICA

Although it is an ancient path established by God, it seems parental blessing and the resultant prosperity of soul were much more common even in American culture as recently as the eighteenth century. I was shocked some time ago when I heard Christian historian David Barton give an American history lecture. I knew it must have taken tremendous courage and integrity for the American colonists to stand up against the most powerful empire in the world at the time, Great Britain, to establish a new nation. I realized they must have felt a great sense of destiny and calling to do so.

I assumed that to possess the courage, character, and settled sense of identity and destiny that it took to found a new nation, most of these early Americans had to have been seasoned veterans of life, people at least in their fifties and sixties. I was shocked to learn that several founding leaders who are household names now were in their teens or early twenties when they performed the acts for which they are now famous.

Perhaps most notable was John Quincy Adams. He apparently began his diplomatic career at age fourteen when he accompanied Francis Dana, whom the Continental Congress had appointed US Minister to Russia, as his secretary and interpreter of French. The two were on an official mission to Russia designed to secure diplomatic recognition of the newly founded United States. Adams was later appointed US Minister to Holland when he was still in his twenties.[4]

Betsy Ross was only twenty-four when she is believed to have created the first official American flag. Then there were Alexander Hamilton, James Monroe, James Madison, John Marshall, and the French Marquis de Lafayette, who were all between the ages of nineteen and twenty-five when they played significant roles in the American Revolutionary War.[5]

How many fourteen-year-olds would you be willing to send overseas as a secretary and interpreter for a diplomat? If you ask your average fourteen-year-old about his purpose and destiny, you will probably hear about video games, TV shows, and goals to be rich and "have fun." Two hundred years ago people commonly practiced law and medicine, started businesses, and got married at ages sixteen, seventeen, and eighteen.

Here is a scary thought: How many of the thirty-year-olds you know would you be willing to send overseas as an ambassador from your nation? Oftentimes even many thirty-year-olds today do not display the integrity and sense of destiny that were evident in fourteen-year-olds two hundred years ago. Why not? We have departed from God's ancient paths.

Apparently even in the United States two hundred years ago there was a different sort of confidence, maturity, and character in young people than there is today. Why? I believe the answer rests in impartation of blessing from parents to children, a tradition that was still more intact even in American culture two centuries ago. Before the Industrial Revolution of the 1840s every child had a *father*, a *family*, and a *future*.

Families ate meals together every day, and parents blessed their children regularly. Two centuries ago parents prepared their children to fulfill a destiny, not just to have a job.

Today many people are wanderers on the planet simply trying to pay their bills and keep their marriages and families from disaster. They're searching for significance and purpose and are plagued by a continual restlessness. They constantly wonder, "Am I really loved or valuable? Am I doing anything that is truly significant or meaningful?" These deep questions of the soul were meant to be answered by God through powerful impartations of identity and destiny that come when a child's father and mother bless him at critical stages in life.

BLESSING AND CURSING
IMPACT GENERATIONS

As we have discussed, family blessing or cursing often determines the course of a child's destiny not for one generation but for many generations. Both blessing and cursing are seeds that will reproduce after their kind for generations. Noel and Phyl Gibson in their book *Evicting Demonic Squatters and Breaking Bondages* discovered some very interesting statistics about two American families when they traced them over two hundred years.

> Max Jukes was an atheist who married a godless woman. Some 560 descendants were traced: 310 died as paupers, 150 became criminals, 7 of them murderers, 100 were known drunkards, and half the women were prostitutes. The descendants of Max Jukes cost the United States government more than 1.25 million dollars in 19th century dollars.
>
> Jonathan Edwards was a contemporary of Max Jukes. He was a committed Christian who gave God first place in his life. He married a godly young lady, and some 1,394 descendants were traced: 295 graduated from college, of

whom 13 became college presidents and 65 became professors, 3 were elected as United States senators, 3 as state governors and others were sent as ministers to foreign countries, 30 were judges, 100 were lawyers, one the dean of an outstanding law school, 56 practiced as physicians, one was the dean of a medical school, 75 became officers in the military, 100 were well-known missionaries, preachers and prominent authors, another 80 held some form of public office, of whom 3 were mayors of large cities, 1 was the comptroller of the U.S. Treasury, and another was vice president of the United States.[6]

It is amazing that none of Edwards' descendants were ever a liability to the government. Understanding the natural consequences of the choices made within these two families, one can conclude that someone born into the Jukes family would have been more likely to have had a difficult time in marriage and child-rearing than a person born into the Edwards family.

That does not mean the family a person is born into determines his destiny. No matter what a person's family background, he can always choose to make wise, godly choices that will improve his marriage and family relationships. He can choose to establish a lifestyle of blessing that will put his children and future generations on an entirely different track. At any point, it is possible to recognize and break the power of negative generational patterns and leave a godly heritage.

KEY QUESTIONS
ANSWERED BY BLESSING

In the introduction I mentioned that there are seven critical stages in life during which blessing was meant to be imparted within a family. At each of these critical times I believe God intended to answer a key spiritual and emotional question in our hearts. In the next several chapters we will look at each of these critical stages and the deep heart questions answered at these times. Because this is so critical to any parent wanting to establish a culture of blessing in their families, I have included a chart below that summarizes what to expect in each stage.

MAJOR LIFE QUESTIONS BLESSING ANSWERS	
Critical Time of Blessing	**Major Life Questions Answered**
Conception	Am I wanted and *welcome* in this family?
Time in the womb	Am I accepted and safe? Do I *belong* here?
Birth	Am I what you expected and *wanted*? Am I OK, or is something wrong with me? Will anyone *take care* of me?
Early childhood	Is there anyone I can really *trust* to meet my needs? Is there anyone here bigger, stronger, and wiser than me who truly loves and cares about me?
Puberty	Do I have what it takes to be a man/woman? Am I *adequate* to fulfill my calling as an adult?
Marriage	Am I really *lovable*? Will anyone love me and stick with me in covenant long-term?
Older age	Am I *still needed*, and have I really accomplished anything significant in my life?

Chapter 4

BLESSING YOUR CHILD
AT CONCEPTION

W<small>E WILL SPEND</small> the next several chapters looking at each critical time of blessing. Before we dig deep into this topic, I want to remind you that there is an intense spiritual battle over whose message of identity and destiny will be imparted deep inside the heart of a child. If parents are not aware of this battle, the devil will use them to inadvertently impart his message of worthlessness and purposelessness into the hearts of their children. So it is important that as parents you remain focused on God's truth about your child—and about yourself. God's message of love and value is just as true for you. It is often out of our own sense of worthlessness that we impart the same ungodly message to our children.

KEY ROLE PLAYER

Satan starts at the very beginning trying to impact a child's image of identity and destiny. That is why the first critical time of blessing is at conception, and God wants to use both parents as His agents of blessing at this strategic time. The father and mother play an equally important role in creating a safe and blessed environment into which a child may enter. Both parents are equally necessary and equally responsible to bless the child at this time.

KEY QUESTION TO BE ANSWERED

As I mentioned in the previous chapter, at each critical time of blessing there is a key question being answered in the heart of the child. Again, either God or Satan can answer the question through the messages parents impart. I believe that the primary question being answered at the time of conception is: *Am I wanted and welcome in this family?*

Satan and his kingdom of darkness, of course, want parents to answer this question by saying, "*No*, you are not welcome. We don't want you. No one wants you. We didn't want a child. You are a nuisance, a bother, and an intrusion into our lives. You are a mistake, just a product of lust with no purpose and no destiny."

God's answer is just the opposite. He wants parents to convey: "*Yes*, you are completely welcome. We want you and are anticipating your birth with joy. You have a place in this family, and you are a great blessing to us. God has given you a unique purpose and destiny, and we will do everything possible to help protect and guide you to fulfill that purpose."

To be blessed or cursed at the time of conception would mean the following types of things.

Blessing at conception

1. Both parents want the child and anticipate the birth with great joy.

2. The parents are in a legitimate covenant of marriage.

3. The conception occurs in love and not in lust.

Cursing at conception

1. Either or both parents do not anticipate and do not want the child.

2. Either parent resents the conception and sees the child as an intrusion.

3. The conception occurs outside of the covenant of marriage.

4. The conception occurs in lust and not in love.

POTENTIAL CONSEQUENCES OF BLESSING AND CURSING

When a child is blessed at the time of conception, the parents are giving God authority to impart His message into the child's heart from the very beginning. This means that right at the time of conception, a strong sense of being valued, loved, wanted, accepted, and welcomed will be present. A clear sense of purpose and destiny is released to the child from the start. When the conception is blessed, the parents are recognizing that this child is not an accident. Rather, God has chosen to create and release that specific child at that specific time into that specific family to fulfill a divine purpose and destiny.

Another key benefit of the parents' blessing at the time of conception is that through this act the father and mother place a spiritual hedge of protection around the child that blocks demonic access to the child while he is in the womb. Many parents do not realize that the marriage covenant creates a spiritual hedge of protection around the conception of a child and his or her ongoing growth in the womb. When parents conceive a child outside the protective hedge of marriage, the unborn child is potentially exposed to whatever demonic spirits may be present at that time.

We will examine this concept in more detail later in this chapter, but I wanted to point this out as a reminder of the power of the marriage covenant. There was a time not terribly long ago when it was considered immoral for a couple to have a sexual relationship outside marriage. Today premarital sex and cohabitation have become so common that many people consider it normal behavior. They have no idea the devastating generational consequences these choices bring.

When I began to study more deeply what the Bible had to say about the consequences of conception outside of the protective hedge of marriage, one of the first scriptures I encountered was Deuteronomy 23:2: "No one of illegitimate birth shall enter the assembly of the LORD; none of his descendants, even to the tenth generation, shall enter the assembly of the LORD."

This seemed to be quite a severe consequence, so I asked the Lord what this verse meant. I wondered if God was saying that He would not receive a person of illegitimate birth in His congregation for ten generations. When I prayed about this, I clearly heard the Father say, "It is not that I will not accept the person of illegitimate birth, but rather that the enemy has a legal right to keep him out of My congregation for up to ten generations. I am willing to accept anyone who comes to me in the name of Jesus."

This is a devastating consequence if through one act of sexual sin demonic spirits have a legal right to afflict up to ten future generations of people. If each generation has only four children, then by the tenth generation more than one million people would have been affected. So through one act of sexual immorality the enemy has the potential to devastate more than a million people. This, in my opinion, is a highly effective scheme of destruction. If I were the devil, I would work diligently on this plan, and it seems he is doing just that. According to the Centers for Disease Control and Prevention, roughly 40 percent of births in the United States are to unmarried women.[1]

THE STRONGMAN PRINCIPLE

Many years ago I discovered a biblical principle that is critical for every parent to understand. I have come to call it the "strongman principle." Whether they realize it or not, all parents are "strongmen." They are gatekeepers, as it were, for their children. Through the choices parents make, they expose their children either to the things of God or the things of the devil. This may seem unfair, but it is indeed how life on Planet Earth is set up.

The Bible talks about the strongman principle in the Book of Matthew. Jesus said, "How can anyone enter the strong man's house and carry off his property, unless he first binds the strong man? And then he will plunder his house" (Matt. 12:29).

In this passage Jesus was explaining how to expel demonic spirits. He seems to imply that there is a hierarchy of demonic spirits with which one must deal. The lesser ones seem to be protected by the authority of the stronger ones. So if one attempts to expel a demonic spirit that is lower in the chain of command and abiding under the protection of a stronger demon, the authority of that stronger demon allows that spirit to remain in place.

Consequently one must first find the highest-ranking spirit operating in the situation, which in this verse Jesus calls the "strong man." Only when you bind him is it possible to eliminate all the lower-ranking demons and clean the house. I have personally found this principle to be true, and I know many seasoned deliverance ministers who also attest to this.

As I meditated on this passage one day, it occurred to me that the strongman principle works exactly the same when Satan and his demonic spirits are trying to invade your house. The Greek word translated "house" is *oikos*. But in Matthew 12:29, *oikos* does not refer to a physical dwelling place but to the family. For example, in Acts 16:30–31 the Philippian jailer asked Paul what he must do to be saved. Paul said, "Believe in the Lord Jesus, and you will be saved, you and your household [*oikos*]." Obviously, Paul was not saying the physical structure in which the jailer lived would be saved; he was referring to the man's family and extended household.

So when the enemy comes to plunder your house (*oikos*), he is after your family. His purpose is to devastate your marriage, children, and grandchildren. But to do so, he must first bind the strongman. Who is the strongman of your house? The husband is the strongman to the wife, and both parents are strongmen to the children. *Thus in any area of life in which the enemy can bind or access the parents, he can bind or access the children.*

Satan, being a legalist, understands the universal laws of God and the principles of authority. Thus the devil and every demonic spirit know they cannot directly attack children who abide under the authority of their parents; they must go through the parents to get to the kids. Sadly, if parents are blind to Satan's devices, or if they don't understand their role as strongmen, the enemy may get direct access to the hearts and lives of their children through the doors they unwittingly open (Hosea 4:6).

Let me give you a few practical examples of the strongman principle at work. Suppose a father is driving recklessly with his three-year-old son and two-year-old daughter strapped in the backseat. Just as he turns around a sharp curve, a rabbit runs out in front of the car, causing him to swerve and lose control of the car. The car crashes, and the father and his two young children are killed.

In this case it is clear that the two children died because of their father's actions. It was not the children's fault; they had no choice in the matter. A father driving his car recklessly with his children inside exposes them to danger. The father was charged by God to serve and protect his children, but in this case he did not do so. This is unfair, but it is how life works. Children are indeed exposed to benefit or destruction based on their parents' choices.

Let me give you a couple of other physical examples of the responsibility parents have to discern danger and establish protective boundaries for their children. Toddlers in general have no true understanding of gravity, traffic, or poison. God, being very smart, placed protective agents in the lives of these children who are supposed to have more understanding of the dangers in the world than the children. Of course these agents are called parents.

Therefore a loving and wise parent establishes protective boundaries to restrain unaware children from harm. Wise parents may build a fence with a locked gate around the lawn of their home to restrain a small child from running into a busy street and risk getting hit by a car. Likewise the parent may place a gate at the top of a staircase to the basement to keep a toddler from falling down the stairs and injuring himself. A parent may place potentially poisonous medicines in a locked cabinet to prevent a child from drinking lethal substances. These locked gates and cabinets may be inconvenient for the parents but are there for the sake of the children.

Suppose, however, that parents did not understand the danger of traffic, gravity, or poison. Those parents likely would not establish or maintain protective boundaries for their children to guard their children from these threats. It's clear that the children of these uninformed parents are at great risk of harm, and many will perish simply because their parents lack understanding. I believe this paints an accurate picture of the situation in many families today.

Most parents understand the importance of establishing physical boundaries for their children, but many seem oblivious to the need for them to also establish the spiritual boundaries to protect their children. Through the years I have heard a certain type of testimony again and again. A father on a business trip finds himself alone in his hotel room facing a lot of pressure from his work and feeling a little unappreciated.

He turns on the television and begins to channel surf. Soon he has stumbled across a pornographic movie and is enticed to watch it. Afterward he feels guilty, and the next morning he asks God to forgive him.

Question: Has this father's choices affected anyone other than himself? Answer: Absolutely! As a father he is a spiritual strongman to his wife and children. Satan can access a godly parent's child in the area in which he can bind the parent. Yet the father in my example has no understanding of his role as a spiritual strongman for his children. Therefore he is both surprised and devastated a few weeks later when he and his wife learn their thirteen-year-old daughter has been "sexting" (sending and receiving text messages with lewd photos attached) with boys in the church youth group.

"How could this have happened?" he wonders. The enemy succeeded in binding the father in the area of lust, and through that opened door Satan accessed the daughter. In 1 Peter 5:8 the Bible tells us that our adversary, Satan, prowls around like a roaring lion, seeking someone to devour. Without realizing it, this father opened a door that allowed the roaring lion to devour his daughter. It is important for this father to now close the spiritual door he opened by repenting of his actions before God; then he must take back the ground in his life and in his children's lives that he gave over to the enemy.

God established many protective boundaries for families by means of ceremonies, traditions, and cultural values, but our society has, for the most part, abandoned them because we have not understood their purpose. Many of these ceremonies, traditions, and values were thought to be purposeless and inconvenient, even by Christians. Parents just did not realize that these traditions created or maintained a hedge of spiritual protection around their families.

In reality, a family is a spiritual entity, not just a collection of people living under one roof. There is a type of spiritual glue that unites a family, just as there is a type of "nuclear glue" that bonds the particles of an atom together. When an atom is split, it does not affect just that one atom. The split initiates a chain reaction with far-reaching and often devastating consequences, as this process produces energy that can drive the explosion of nuclear weapons. A similar principle is at work in a family. There is spiritual protection within the confines of a family, and if there is a break, the consequences are far-reaching and potentially devastating.

I promised I would go into more detail about the importance of the marriage covenant. Many people seem to think marriage is a somewhat antiquated concept, nothing more than a legal piece of paper. This is not at all true spiritually. I believe that if a legitimate covenant of marriage ceremony could be recorded with a spiritual video camera, we would see two things happening in the spirit realm. I believe we would see something like the creation of a new atom that previously had not existed.

First, we would see two separate families (atoms), each with their own nuclear glue and spiritual hedge of protection. Then in the ceremony, in a right and healthy way, the young man (one atomic particle) would be severed from his parents (the atom) and a young woman (another atomic particle from a separate atom) would be severed from her parents (a second atom). This is described in Genesis 2:24: "For this reason a man shall leave his father and his mother."

Second, when the pastor or presiding authority proclaims, "By the power vested in me, I now pronounce you husband and wife," I believe that spiritual video camera would record the creation of a brand-new family (atom) that now has its own nuclear glue and spiritual hedge of protection. This part of the process is also described in Genesis 2:24 when it says the man will "be joined to his wife; and they shall become *one flesh*" (emphasis added). I believe the phrase "one flesh" is referring to this newly created spiritual entity.

Let's now put this into the context of the spiritual battle in which we are currently engaged. As mentioned earlier, God's plan is to empower everyone to fulfill his God-given purpose and destiny, while Satan's plan is to destroy everyone's identity and destiny. Hence a spiritual battle rages for access to each person's life from the day of his conception. How well do you think a toddler or, worse yet, a child in the womb can understand spiritual warfare and protect himself from demonic entities? Not at all! The child is defenseless.

So a baby in the womb has no chance to even understand the ravenous lion seeking to destroy his life. God, being real smart, understood this and provided His agents to preserve and protect the life of this child. Again, these agents are called parents. God intended for parents to understand the spiritual threats against their family and their role in establishing a spiritually protective hedge for their children through the covenant of marriage.

Children conceived outside the marriage covenant have no spiritual protection. Even many Christians don't realize that the covenant of marriage *is* the spiritual hedge that protects unborn children from demonic access. It is so much more than a piece of paper.

From a spiritual warfare standpoint, a child conceived outside the covenant of marriage is completely exposed and vulnerable, similar to a child sitting on top of a pile of bricks in a war zone. A child conceived within the protective bounds of marriage, on the other hand, is much like child inside a brick fort in a war zone. If your children are indeed found in a war zone with a brutal enemy seeking to destroy them, would you rather they be enclosed in a fortified brick castle or just sitting on a pile of bricks totally exposed to the enemy?

I have had some teens say to me, "I don't see what's wrong

with sleeping with my girlfriend if we really love each other and we are committed to getting married." They don't realize it, but they've already stated the problem: they don't see what's wrong. Many people *don't see* longer-term or generational consequences to their choices. This is why God gave us written instructions in His Owner's Manual, the Bible.

While some people are busy seeing what it's like to violate God's instructions, they are potentially opening doors to the demonic realm in their own lives and in the lives of their children. Unfortunately most people never do correlate the subsequent fruit in the lives of their children or future generations with the seed they sowed in their generation.

"You mean to tell me, Pastor, that there is a difference between whether I engage in sexual intercourse with my fiancée five minutes before the wedding ceremony or with my wife five minutes after the ceremony?" When young people ask me this, I have had to tell them, "Absolutely—especially if a child is conceived." That wedding ceremony is not just a formality; it is a spiritual reality. It creates a spiritual hedge of protection both for the couple and any children they may conceive. I've seen many people who have violated this principle weep bitterly when they realized the consequences of their selfish choices. I first learned this lesson through a dramatic encounter with one family several years ago.

Freedom for Susan's Son

Susan came up to me during an Ancient Paths Experience I was conducting to talk with me about her five-year-old son, Billy. Though just a young boy, Billy was consumed with an unusual sexual lust. He was continually spouting sexual obscenities. He knew all the latest sexual jokes, and he devoured any type of pornography he could find.

"Worst of all," Susan told me, "a couple of weeks ago I left Billy alone in a room with his one-and-a-half-year-old baby sister. I couldn't have been gone for more than three minutes, and when I returned, I found Billy unclothed and attempting to enter into sexual relationship with his baby sister. It scared me to death."

Susan knew this was not normal behavior for a five-year-old—it's not normal for a child that young to even be so aware of such things. "I don't know where he could have picked up this type of thinking and behavior," Susan cried. "To our knowledge he has never been around people who think or act this way. My husband and I are very careful about the children Billy plays with. He has never been molested. Of course, now no other parents will let their children play with Billy.

"We just don't know what to do. He is a constant embarrassment to me. I can't take him anywhere because I never know what he is going to do or say. I have to continually watch him at home for fear he will molest the baby. We've tried praying for him, taking him to a psychiatrist—everything we know of—but nothing seems to help."

Susan's pastor was sitting with me as Susan described Billy's behavior. The pastor confirmed that the situation was indeed as bad as Susan described and that they had done everything they knew to do. I didn't have any answers for them, so I suggested we pray. As we got quiet before the Lord, I felt the Holy Spirit lead me to ask Susan a series of questions.

"Let's just start at the very beginning of Billy's life," I said. "Can you tell me how your son was conceived?"

Susan sat in silence for several seconds as tears began to stream down her cheeks. "I was not walking with God at that time in my life," she said. "As a matter of fact, I was living a very immoral lifestyle. As close as I can tell, the night Billy was conceived I was with several different men. I have no idea which one is his biological father. I lived this way for another three months or so before I gave my life to the Lord. Since then I have been walking with the Lord and have not been involved in sexual immorality. Shortly after Billy was born, I met my husband, who is a godly man. We married and have been serving the Lord our entire marriage."

As Susan shared this information, the Lord brought to my mind a very strange thought. Perhaps little Billy had actually been demonized by a spirit of sexual lust right at the time of his conception. His current behavior could be a result of the influence of that demonic spirit in his life. I had never before thought of this possibility, yet I felt very strongly that I should mention it to the pastor and to Susan. When I shared this thought, Susan began to weep profusely. "I'm sure that is exactly what happened," she said through her tears.

"Is your son here with you?" I asked

"No, he is at home with his father," Susan replied. "What should we do? I have already repented of the past sexual immorality. How can we get Billy free of the spirit of lust?"

I then explained to Susan and to the pastor the strongman principle and how conceiving a child outside of marriage leaves him vulnerable to demonic attack. Neither the pastor nor Susan had ever realized this before.

I told Susan that she was the strongman and that she had opened the door in her son's life that allowed a demonic spirit to afflict him in the same area she had been bound. Usually good news becomes relevant only when we understand the true impact of the bad news. So I explained to Susan that she not only had authority as a mother to open the door, but she also had authority as a mother and a believer in Jesus Christ to close the same spiritual door and command the demonic spirit to leave her son.

I then asked the pastor if he had any experience with deliverance ministry. He did, so I instructed Susan to have her husband bring Billy to the pastor's office, where she should take the following steps.

1. Renounce the iniquities of fornication, sexual immorality, and lust in her life.

2. Pray to close the door she had opened through her past actions that had allowed the enemy access to her son.

3. Dispatch the iniquity of lust to the cross of Jesus Christ, who died for all our transgressions and iniquities (Isa. 53:4–6).

4. Pray to break the power of that iniquity over the life of her son.

5. Pray to exchange the iniquity of lust in Billy's life for the blessing of sexual and emotional purity that Jesus died for him to receive.

6. Exercise her authority in Christ, and as a strongman (parent) to command the spirit of lust to leave her son immediately and go where Jesus Christ sends it.

7. Ask the Holy Spirit to fill her son with Himself.

Susan and her pastor agreed to have this meeting the following week. Several months later I returned to the same city to speak at another conference. Immediately after my session, Susan excitedly came running up to me with a little boy in tow. "Remember me, remember me?" she exclaimed.

I actually didn't remember her at first because I had spoken at many events since we met. But when she began to explain her situation to me, I immediately remembered her.

"We did what you said," she said. "My husband and I met with our pastor and our son. We followed the steps you outlined, and when we got to the step to command the spirit of lust to leave our son, we saw a visible manifestation of it leaving and a total change in Billy's countenance."

Susan then burst into tears and proclaimed, "I got my son back! He is a normal little five-year-old boy who doesn't know anything about sex. He doesn't remember any of the sexual jokes he used to tell or even understand what those things mean. When we commanded that spirit to leave him, it did, and there was an instant transformation in my son. His countenance instantly changed, and so did his language and behavior. Thank you so much."

Susan was almost beside herself with joy and just couldn't stop thanking the Lord for setting her son free. "I never before would have believed that it was possible for a little boy to be demonized at the moment of conception had it not happened to my son," Susan said, "and had I not seen the consequences of my past iniquity with my own eyes."

BORN THAT WAY?

The experience I had with Susan and her son dramatically demonstrated to me the serious charge parents have to be gatekeepers, or strongmen, in the lives of their children. Once I understood how vulnerable children conceived outside of marriage are to demonic influence, I was able to understand why some people bound in a lifestyle of homosexuality are convinced they were born with that sense of identity.

As a believer I had always thought no one could be born with a homosexual identity; I thought it must have been acquired sometime in childhood. But when ministering to a young man several years ago, I asked him how long he had felt a homosexual identity, and he said he was quite certain he'd had it from birth. As we prayed, I heard the Lord tell me that he was indeed born with that identity, but he was not created that way.

Because his parents were not married when he was conceived and had provided him no spiritual hedge of protection, this young man had been demonized by a sexually perverse spirit while in the womb. So when he said he was born that way, he was indeed correct. After understanding the origin of his homosexual identity, we were able to minister to him and help him obtain deliverance. Since that time I have seen this same scenario play out in many people. It has only reinforced to me the critical importance of parents blessing their children at the time of conception with the spiritual hedge of protection provided by the covenant of marriage.

GOD'S PROTECTIVE MEASURES IN ANCIENT HEBREW CULTURE

As we look at each of the seven critical times of blessing, we will discover that God placed protective measures in the ancient Hebrew culture to ensure that children would receive His message through blessing and not Satan's message through cursing. God's protection usually was established in the form of laws, cultural attitudes, ceremonies, and traditions.[2]

Knowing the critical need for spiritual protection and blessing at the time of conception, God established the following three key protective boundaries in the ancient Hebrew culture.

1. *The Law of Moses.* This required capital punishment for fornication and adultery (any sexual intercourse outside of the protective hedge of the marriage covenant).

2. *The cultural attitude toward children.* Children were seen as a blessing rather than a bother.

3. *The cultural attitude toward marriage.* It was understood to be a covenant and holy unto the Lord.

When I first began to seek the Lord about the protective boundaries He established in biblical Hebrew culture, I was shocked to learn that the Law of Moses was one of those boundaries. I had always seen "the Law" as legalistic, severe, and arbitrary. I had no idea that it was a loving, protective boundary designed to insure children were blessed at conception. I think one of the enemy's most effective strategies is to get us to disconnect the consequences of our choices from the choices themselves. If sex is seen simply as a recreational activity or a choice made between two consenting adults, then the Law of Moses appears to be nothing more than the antiquated arbitrary edict of a vindictive, judgmental God.

When I was just beginning to understand these concepts, I spent a lot of time in prayer. I asked, "Lord, capital punishment is so severe. If we were to apply that standard in the church today, there may be very few people left in the congregation. Why such a severe consequence?"

I then heard the Father say to me, "That was not My severity, son. That was My mercy—for ten generations of children." Then I remembered Deuteronomy 23:2, which talks about the enemy being able to oppress the descendants of those born out of wedlock for up to ten generations. For the first time I began to understand. The individual and generational impact of sin is always in tension in a society. Mercy toward the generation that sinned creates an open door for the enemy to curse and devastate up to ten generations. On the other hand, taking a more severe stance toward the offending generation brings protection and security for the following ten generations.

Just think about it. If in ancient Israel someone could lose his life for committing fornication or adultery, how likely is it that a child would be conceived out of wedlock? There is almost no chance. Today how likely is it that a child would be conceived out of wedlock? In the United States there's about a 40 percent chance in the general population![3] So which is truly merciful? Since there is indeed a tension, we must ask another question: *mercy for whom?* Are we seeking mercy for the offending parents or for the innocent children conceived with no spiritual protection?

I am not suggesting that we return to a legal system requiring capital punishment for fornication and adultery. However, I am suggesting that we as believers understand the consequences of our choices and the purpose of God's protective boundaries. With such understanding I suggest we create within the community of believers a culture of blessing in which people voluntarily limit their sexual behavior to the context of marriage for the sake of blessing their potential children and many future generations.

The second protective measure God placed in biblical Hebrew society was a high cultural value placed on children. Think about it. One of the worst things that could happen to a Hebrew woman was not the conception of a child; it was to be barren. In contrast, in our society many people take drastic measures to prevent conception. Of course, unmarried couples should not be sexually active, but even some married couples pray that they won't become pregnant. Again, this is a completely different cultural attitude from the biblical Hebrews' perspective.

If you were a child in the biblical Hebrew culture, how likely is it that your mom and dad would have tried to prevent your conception? Again, there's almost no chance! Everybody wanted children; they were considered a blessing. God's attitude toward children, embraced by the ancient Hebrew culture, is expressed in Psalm 127:3–5: "Behold, children are a gift of the LORD; the fruit of the womb is a reward. Like arrows in the hand of a warrior, so are the children of one's youth. How blessed is the man whose quiver is full of them."

In our society today how likely is it that the conception of a child would not be welcome news to the parents? There is a great likelihood! Today in Western society a large family is considered an oddity. In general, even among believers, children are not considered a blessing and a reward from God but rather a bother, a burden, a nuisance, and a financial drain on the family. Almost every child would have been blessed and welcomed in biblical Hebrew culture, but this protective cultural attitude has nearly been destroyed in our modern church culture.

The third protective measure for children I saw in biblical Hebrew culture was the cultural sanctity of marriage. In that culture marriage was considered holy unto the Lord (Mal. 2:13–15), and divorce was very rarely practiced. Consequently children could be conceived and could grow in a very stable, secure environment anchored by a married mom and dad. Today, with our high divorce rate, marriage is much less secure, and the family is not as stable an environment.

Because of these three protective measures God established in biblical Hebrew culture, it was very unlikely that a child would have had his or her identity cursed at the time of conception. It is critical for believers today to understand the importance of reestablishing a culture of blessing in our communities. This is how children can have the same protective environment the ancient Hebrews had to ensure their blessing at conception.

In the Blessing Toolbox in this chapter and chapters 5 through 10 I outline practical steps you can take to establish or restore protective boundaries around your family similar to those present in the ancient Hebrew culture. In most cases we cannot restore the same protective boundaries that existed thousands of years ago. However, we can learn God's ancient path principles and implement ceremonies, traditions, and practices appropriate to our own culture that will restore the intention of God's ancient path and create a modern-day culture of blessing.

••• BLESSING TOOLBOX •••

This Blessing Toolbox provides practical tools you can use to create a culture of blessing first within your own family and then within your community. For each critical time of blessing there are two sets of tools to help you both repair damage done from the lack of blessing in the past (remedial) and to establish a culture of blessing in your family now (preventative).

REMEDIAL PRAYERS TO BREAK THE CURSE

If you already have a child conceived outside the protective hedge of the covenant of marriage

I encourage you to follow the steps below. You may pray steps one through three without your child present. While it's not essential, I suggest you pray steps four through seven in the presence of your child. If you are married, it is important for you and your spouse to pray through these steps together as spiritual gatekeepers over your child. If you are a single parent, pray *the same prayers on your own.*

1. Renounce the iniquity.

> *Father, I acknowledge this day that I have been bound in the iniquity of lust, fornication, sexual immorality,* [and any other sexual iniquity that God brings to your mind such as masturbation, pornography, homosexuality, sexual perversion, voyeurism, etc.]. *I renounce this iniquity and ask You to forgive me by the blood of Jesus for allowing it to operate in my life.*

If you recognize that the same iniquity operated in your father, grandfather, or past generations, then pray the following:

Father, I recognize that my father [or grandfather] *was bound in the iniquity of fornication, adultery, sexual immorality, pornography,* [or whatever the iniquity]. *He opened the door for the enemy to enter our family. Today I forgive my father* [or grandfather or other ancestors] *for entertaining this iniquity and opening the door to it in our family. Jesus Christ shed His blood to release me from this iniquity, and today I apply His blood to terminate the power of this iniquity in my life. Amen.*

2. Pray to close the open spiritual door.

Father, I recognize today that I opened the door for the enemy to access my son/daughter in the area of lust, sexual sin, fornication, immorality, [or anything else the Lord brings to your mind]. *I had authority to open this spiritual door, and I have authority to close it. So this day, in the name of Jesus Christ, I close every door I opened in the life of my son/daughter to every sexual iniquity. I terminate the function of this iniquity in my family in this generation, and I declare that it stops now in my life. In Jesus's name, this iniquity has no authority to function in my family in any future generation.*

3. Send the iniquity to the cross of Christ.

I now dispatch the iniquity of lust, sexual sin, fornication, immorality, [and anything else the Lord has brought to your mind] *to the cross of Jesus Christ. Jesus died to take that iniquity upon Himself on the cross, and I now release that iniquity to the cross of Christ.*

4. Break the power of the iniquity over your child's life.

In the name of Jesus Christ I now break the power of the iniquity of lust, sexual sin, fornication, immorality, [and anything else the Lord has brought to your mind] *over* [your child's name]. *I declare that Jesus died to take this iniquity upon Himself on the cross, and this iniquity will no longer function in* [your child's name]*'s life.*

5. Release the blessing Jesus Christ died to purchase into the life of your child.

I now release upon [your child's name] *the blessing Jesus Christ died to purchase for him/her. I now declare over you,* [your child's name], *that you will know nothing all the days of your life but emotional purity, sexual purity, and marital fidelity. Any children you will ever conceive will always be conceived within the protective hedge of the covenant of marriage from this day forth.*

I bless the day of your conception and declare that you are wanted and welcome in this family. You are your heavenly Father's legitimate son/daughter, and He chose you to be born for such a time as this. You were conceived right on time, and you are supposed to be here. God chose to give you life and to give you to us as a gift. We receive your life as a unique gift from God to our family, and we thank God for making you a part of our family in His unique and special timing. You are absolutely unique, and no one else can accomplish or fulfill your purpose on earth. I bless your life, your spirit, your health, your destiny and purpose, and your place in our family.

May you be blessed in all you are and all you do from the day of your conception onward!

6. Command any attending demonic spirit to leave your child and never return.

In the name of Jesus Christ I now command the spirit of [name or function of the demon] *to leave my son/daughter now and never return. You have no more authority over his/her life. Leave and go to the place Jesus Christ sends you.*

7. Ask God to fill your child with His Holy Spirit.

Father, please fill [your child's name] *with Your Holy Spirit right now. I bless him/her with the infilling of Your Holy Spirit, in Jesus's name.*

If you have adopted children who you know or suspect were conceived outside of the covenant of marriage

Remember that God has given you, as an adoptive parent, spiritual authority over your adoptive children. Therefore you can pray to break the iniquity of sexual immorality in their lives. The steps to take in prayer would be similar to those above.

1. Renounce the iniquity.

Father, we recognize this day that [your child's name]*'s biological father and mother may have been bound in the iniquity of lust, fornication, sexual immorality,* [and any other sexual iniquity that you know of or that God brings to your mind]. *With the authority of Jesus Christ, as* [your child's name]*'s parents, we cancel the right of this iniquity to function in* [your child's name]*'s life or in any future generations in his/her bloodline. We forgive* [your child's name]*'s biological father and mother and all past generations for their participation in this iniquity, and by the blood of Jesus Christ we cut off this iniquity of sexual sin in this generation. Amen.*

2. Pray to close the open spiritual door.

Father, we recognize today that [your child's name]*'s biological parents may have opened a spiritual door to our son/daughter in the area of lust, sexual sin, fornication, immorality,* [and anything else the Lord brings to your mind]. *With the authority of Jesus Christ as* [your child's name]*'s parents, we now close this spiritual door to all sexual iniquity in* [your child's name]*'s life in this generation and in all future generations. We terminate this day any legal or spiritual authority granted to Satan or demonic spirits by* [your child's name]*'s biological father or mother, grandparents, or any past generations. As his father and mother, we dedicate* [your child's name] *solely to Jesus Christ and declare that he/she shall belong to and serve God in righteousness all the days of his/her life. Amen.*

3. Pray steps four through seven above over your child.

1. You may also want to pray the following over your adopted child:

Father, even as we have been adopted and grafted into Your family by the blood of Jesus Christ, we reaffirm our choice to receive [your child's name] *to be adopted and fully grafted into our family.* [Your child's name], *we bless you as our son/daughter and declare over you that you are welcome and belong in our family. Many children's parents don't have a choice about which children will be a part of their family, but we did have a choice, and we purposely chose you to be our son/daughter. We chose you because you are so special and so uniquely valuable that the first time we heard of you, we loved you, we wanted you, and we knew that God wanted you to be a part of our family.*

So today we declare that you are our beloved son/ daughter in whom we are well pleased. We love you. We receive you. We want you to know that we will treat you just as our heavenly Father treats us as His adopted sons and daughters. We will never leave you or forsake you, and you will always be our son/ daughter whom we love. We bless you and declare that you shall prosper in all of your life, in Jesus's name, amen.

PREVENTATIVE PRAYERS TO RELEASE THE BLESSING

Bless the day of your future child's conception.

Father, we give You permission to give us the gift of children as You see fit. Lord, we acknowledge that children are a gift from You, and we gladly accept this gift of a child from Your hand. Father, we bless in advance the spirit of our child even at the moment of conception, and we declare that our child will prosper and be blessed according to Your purpose all the days of his or her life. We declare, Father, that any children you choose to send us are welcome and belong in our family, and we bless them with a strong sense of being loved, valued, and welcomed from the very moment of conception onward, in Jesus's name, amen.

Bless the day of your present child's conception.

Father, we thank You for the gift that [your child's name] *is to us.* [Your child's name], *we bless the day of your conception and declare that you are wanted and welcome in this family. You are your heavenly Father's legitimate son/daughter, and He chose you to be born for such a time as this. You were conceived right on time, and you are supposed to be here. God chose to give you life and to give you to us as a gift. We receive your life as a unique gift from God to our family, and we thank God for making you a part of our family in His unique and special timing. You are absolutely unique, and no one else can accomplish or fulfill your purpose on earth. We bless your life, your spirit, your health, your destiny and purpose, and your place in our family. May you be blessed in all you are and all you do from the day of your conception forward! In Jesus's name, amen.*

Chapter 5

BLESSING YOUR CHILD
IN THE WOMB

L ET'S NOW TURN to the second critical time God intended
for a child to receive his parent's blessing: in the womb. This
second key phase entails the entire gestational period—from
conception through birth. In the past some people thought
unborn children were little inanimate lumps of flesh with no
thoughts or feelings. Of course, we know from Scripture that
God created each child and breathed the human spirit into him
at the moment of conception. The Bible makes it clear that God
had plans for us before we were even conceived.

> I will give thanks to You, *for I am fearfully and wonder-
> fully made:* Wonderful are Your works, and my soul knows
> it very well. My frame was not hidden from You, when I
> was made in secret, and skillfully wrought in the depths
> of the earth; Your eyes have seen my unformed sub-
> stance; and in Your book were written the days that were
> ordained for me, when as yet there was not one of them.
> —PSALM 139:14–16, EMPHASIS ADDED

> Thus says the LORD, your Redeemer, and *the one who
> formed you from the womb.*
> —ISAIAH 44:24, EMPHASIS ADDED

> But when *God, who had set me apart even from my
> mother's womb* and called me through His grace, was
> pleased to reveal His Son to me so that I might preach
> Him among the Gentiles.
> —GALATIANS 1:15–16, EMPHASIS ADDED

So we see that God created and released us to be conceived at just the correct time. Whether or not our parents followed God's design and were married at the time of our conception, not one of us is an accident. God knew exactly when we would be born, and He had a plan for our lives long before our parents even met.

I was in a meeting once, and a young mother came up to me with tears in her eyes and said, "I was violently raped when I was fifteen years old and conceived my oldest son as a result. Do you think that it was God's will and plan for that man to rape me so that my son could be born?"

"No, of course not!" I responded. I explained that rape is never God's will or plan for anyone. What that rapist did to her was sin, motivated by Satan and not by God. However, God uses even the evil works of the devil to ultimately bless and benefit us. Paul tells us in Romans 8:28 that "God causes all things to work together for good to those who love God, to those who are called according to His purpose."

So we see that while God is not the author of all circumstances, He certainly is the master of all circumstances. In this case of a rape, the enemy may have been able to pervert how the child was conceived, but he could not thwart the ultimate purpose of God in the life of the mother or the child. God knew this tragic rape would occur, so even though the child was not conceived in the way He intended, God still created the child and had a purpose and destiny in mind for him.

It is beyond the scope of this book to delve deep into explaining the sovereignty of God, why injustice occurs, or how evil operates in the earth. For a thorough treatment of this subject, please see my book *If God Is in Control, Then Why...? Trusting a Just God in an Unjust World*, particularly chapters 2 and 3.[1]

KEY ROLE PLAYER

When a child is in the womb, the mother is obviously the key role player in the child's life. While the attitudes, words, and emotions of the mother profoundly impact the growing child, the father also has a powerful responsibility to bless not only his child but also his wife. How the father treats his wife during this time can have a significant effect on the growing child as well.

KEY QUESTION TO BE ANSWERED

The key questions to be answered by either God or the devil through the words and emotions of the parents are: *Am I accepted and safe? Do I belong here?*

Of course, Satan and the kingdom of darkness want to use parents to answer this question with a resounding, "*No*, you are not accepted. This place is not safe for you, and you shouldn't even be here. We don't want you. You are an intrusion, a bother, and a nuisance. Someone has played a cruel joke on you and deposited you in this hostile environment where you are not wanted and are totally alone to be tormented by demonic spirits. Maybe you will die or just somehow go away and stop bothering us."

Again, God's answer is just the opposite. He wants to use both parents to convey: "You are accepted, wanted, and safe here. God made a reservation for you, and we have been waiting with great expectation and anticipation for the exciting news of your arrival. We will love you, protect you, care for you, nurture you, and bless you in every way possible. We can't wait for you to be born so we can see with our own eyes the beautiful gift God has given us."

BLESSING AND CURSING
YOUR CHILD IN THE WOMB

The identity of an unborn child can be either blessed or cursed from the moment of conception until birth. Of course, it was God's plan for the child to be blessed during the entire gestational period, but this is not always what happens. So what might blessing and cursing in the womb look like?

Blessing your child in the womb may include:

1. The parents providing a spiritually protected environment for the child by being within the protective hedge of the covenant of marriage

2. Conveying to the child he is wanted, accepted, and received

3. Being excited about the gift God has given you in the conception of a child

4. The mother being free of emotional stress and turmoil in her life

5. The mother and father providing an environment of love, nurture, and joy

Cursing a child in the womb may involve such things as:

1. The parents leaving the child vulnerable to demonic attack by not providing the spiritual protection afforded by the covenant of marriage

2. Conveying to the unborn child he is unwanted and unwelcome

3. Feeling the child is a bother or an intrusion into the mother's life

4. The mother living in an environment of emotional stress, turmoil, fear, or anxiety

5. The parents not communicating nurture, love, or value to the child

6. The mother attempting to abort the child

THE AMAZING EXPERIENCE OF AN UNBORN CHILD

Not only does Scripture tell us that children need to be blessed in the womb, but also the science of prenatal medicine and psychology confirms this. The most interesting and informative book I have ever read on this topic was written by a prenatal psychiatrist named Dr. Thomas Verny. Titled *The Secret Life of the Unborn Child*, this book confirms that parents can either bless or curse the identity of children in the womb and that such impartations may affect the child's self-image for the rest of his life. An unborn child is not just an inanimate "fetus." He is a real person who feels and whose identity and self-perception are strongly shaped by his parents' words, emotions, and attitudes. Dr. Verny writes:

> We now know that the unborn child is an aware, reacting human being who from the sixth month on (and perhaps even earlier) leads an active emotional life. Along with this startling finding we have made these discoveries:
>
> - The fetus can see, hear, experience, taste, and, on a primitive level, even learn *in utero* (that is, in the uterus—before birth). Most importantly, he can *feel*—not with an adult's sophistication, but feel nonetheless.
>
> - A corollary to this discovery is that what a child feels and perceives begins shaping his attitudes and expectations about himself. Whether he ultimately sees himself and, hence, acts as a

happy or sad, aggressive or meek, secure or anxiety-ridden person depends, in part, on the messages he gets about himself in the womb.

- The chief source of those messages is the child's mother. *This does not mean every fleeting worry, doubt or anxiety a woman has rebounds on her child.* What matters are deep persistent *patterns* of feeling. Chronic anxiety or a wrenching ambivalence about motherhood can leave a deep scar on an unborn child's personality. On the other hand, such life-enhancing emotions as joy, elation, and anticipation can contribute significantly to the emotional development of a healthy child.[2]

Dr. Verny says his book "is based on the discovery that the unborn child is a *feeling, remembering, aware* being, and because he is, what happens to him—what happens to all of us—in the nine months between conception and birth molds and shapes personality, drives, and ambitions in very important ways."[3]

Not only are children in the womb impacted emotionally, but Dr. Verny also cites several stories of children learning words, phrases, foreign words, and even musical scores while still in the womb. He tells one notable story of a gifted philharmonic conductor, Boris Brott, who had been asked in a radio interview when he had first become interested in music.

He [Brott] hesitated for a moment and said, "You know, this may sound strange, but music has been a part of me since before birth." Perplexed, the interviewer asked him to explain.

"Well," said Brott, "as a young man, I was mystified by this unusual ability I had—to play certain pieces sight unseen. I'd be conducting a score for the first time and, suddenly, the cello line would jump out at me; I'd know the flow of the piece even before I turned the page of the score. One day, I mentioned this to my mother, who is a professional cellist. I thought she'd be intrigued because it was always the cello line that was so distinct in my mind. She was; but when she heard what the pieces were, the mystery quickly solved itself. All the scores I knew sight unseen were the ones she had played while she was pregnant with me.[4]

As believers, we know that God breathes the human spirit into a child right at the time of conception. Dr. Verny quotes research that again confirms that parents can bless or curse a child's identity from the time of conception on. Referring to the unborn child, Dr. Verny states:

> He can sense and react not only to large, undifferentiated emotions such as love and hate, but also to more shaded complex feeling states like ambivalence and ambiguity.
>
> Precisely at what moment his brain cells acquire this ability is still unknown. One group of investigators believes *something like consciousness exists from the very first moments of conception.* As evidence, they point to the thousands of perfectly healthy women who repeatedly abort spontaneously. There is speculation that in the first weeks—perhaps even hours—after conception, the fertilized ovum possesses enough self-awareness to sense rejection and enough will to act on it.[5]

So we see that the identity of children can be blessed or cursed by spiritual, emotional, verbal, and physical impartations from their parents even as tiny babies in the womb. Dr. Verny's research further demonstrates that children in the womb are more sensitive than adults to the emotions and communication of the mother and father.

An adult, and to a lesser degree a child, has had time to develop defenses and responses. He can soften or deflect the impact of experience. An unborn child cannot. What affects him does so directly. That's why maternal emotions etch themselves so deeply on his psyche and why their tug remains so powerful later in life. Major personality characteristics seldom change. If optimism is engraved on the mind of an unborn child, it will take a great deal of adversity later to erase it.[6]

Dr. Verny goes on to explain that when pregnant women do not communicate with their unborn children, it feels to that child much like being alone in a room for six, seven, or eight months without any emotional or intellectual connection.

He [the unborn child] has to feel loved and wanted just as urgently—perhaps even more urgently—than we do. He has to be talked to and thought of; otherwise his spirit and often his body, too, begin wilting....By and large, the personality of the unborn child a woman bears is a function of the quality of mother-child communication, and also of its specificity. If the communication was abundant, rich and, most important, nurturing, the chances are very good that the baby will be robust, healthy and happy.

This communication is an important part of bonding.[7]

Blessing a Child in the Womb

So we see that secular prenatal psychology confirms that a child needs to receive blessing, nurturing, and love during the time spent in the womb. Both father and mother can bless their children in the womb by speaking to them, praying over them, nurturing them, loving them, and basically treating them like real people even though they cannot physically see them yet. It is the parents' privilege and responsibility to communicate to their child God's message that "you are accepted, loved, and welcome. This is a safe place for you to be, to grow, and to receive our love."

While the mother is the primary person God is using to impart His message to her unborn child, the father is also a very important factor in the blessing of the child. Dr. Verny explains.

> Everything that affects her (the mother) affects him (the child). And nothing affects her as deeply or hits with such lacerating impact as worries about her husband (or partner). Because of that, few things are more dangerous to a child, emotionally and physically, than a father who abuses or neglects his pregnant wife.
>
> An equally vital factor in the child's emotional well-being is his father's commitment to the marriage.... For obvious psychological reasons, a man is at something of a disadvantage here. The child is not an organic part of him. But not all the physical impediments of pregnancy are insurmountable. Something as ordinary as talking is a good example: A child hears his father's voice in utero, and there is solid evidence that hearing that voice makes a big emotional difference. In cases where a man talked to his child in utero using short soothing words, the newborn was able to pick out his father's voice in a room even in the first hour or two of life. More than pick it out, he responds to it emotionally. If he is crying, for instance, he'll stop. That familiar soothing sound tells him he is safe.[8]

Several years ago a friend of mine told me a story about his unborn grandson that confirmed the value of blessing a child in the womb. Having understood the critical value of blessing his grandson in the womb, my friend John taught his daughter and son-in-law to speak blessing over their baby from the day they discovered the pregnancy. John also prayed and spoke words of blessing, love, and nurture to the baby every time he was around his daughter.

He would frequently kneel down and speak directly to his grandson in the womb. "Hello, little one," he'd say. "This is your grandfather. I love you! You are so precious to me. You are a gift from God to us, and I can't wait until you are born and I can see you, hold you, kiss your little face, and look into your eyes and tell you how much I love you. You are a mighty man of God who will shake nations in your lifetime."

John was at the hospital the day his grandson was born. After the baby was cleaned up, the nurse handed him to his father and mother to love and hold. When the baby was handed back to the nurse, he began crying. John asked if he might hold his new grandson. The nurse handed the baby to John. He cuddled him, looked into his eyes, and began to say, "Hello, little one. This is your grandfather. I love you! You are so precious to me. You are a gift from God to us."

John said the moment he began to speak, the baby stopped crying and looked up into his eyes. John said it was obvious that the baby recognized the voice that had been speaking to him for the last eight months. John's grandson responded to the familiar voice and seemed to feel safe, secure, and at peace in the loving arms of the grandfather he had never seen but whose blessing he had been receiving all his life in the womb.

Since John shared his story with me many years ago, I have heard similar stories many times from young fathers and mothers who also understood their privilege and responsibility to bless their unborn child. Such blessing has the potential to create a strong sense of inner security and peace in the heart of the child that will last all his life.

Scripture also records the recognition and blessing of children in the womb in the interaction between Mary and her older relative Elizabeth. Mary the mother of Jesus went to visit Elizabeth. "When Elizabeth heard Mary's greeting, the baby leaped in her womb; and Elizabeth was filled with the Holy Spirit. And she cried out with a loud voice and said, 'Blessed are you among women, and blessed is the fruit of your womb! And how it has happened to me, that the mother of my Lord would come to me? *For behold, when the sound of your greeting reached my ears, the baby leaped in my womb for joy*" (Luke 1:41–44, emphasis added).

Cursing a Child in the Womb

Just as a child can be blessed in the womb, so also can the identity of a child be cursed in the womb. Many years ago as I was seeking the Lord, He led me to a key scripture about the long-lasting effects cursing a child's identity in the womb can have in people's lives. The psalmist David wrote, "The wicked are estranged from the womb; these who speak lies go astray from birth" (Ps. 58:3).

At first I thought this scripture could not apply to me or to any believer because we are not the "wicked" but the redeemed. But after conducting a short word study, I found that the Hebrew term translated "wicked" in this verse is *rasha*. This word, of course, means evil or impious, but some of the expanded meanings really caught my attention, including: "to be in a restless, unquiet state; tossed with various evil passions, distracted by many forms of wickedness, and having no peace of conscience, violent commotion within."[9]

As I read this, I realized this word might apply to many people I have met, people who in their adult lives find themselves in a restless, disquieted state of soul, distracted and tossed to and fro by many passions.

The Hebrew word translated "estranged" is *zuwr*. This word can also mean "to be alienated, turned aside, to be treated as an enemy, or made to feel illegitimate, or of another family."[10] The phrase that really caught my attention was "of another family." This feeling could be imparted to a child in the womb if he is made to feel like an enemy or as though he does not belong in the family. The unborn child could be made to feel, "Someone has played a cruel joke on me by placing me in this hostile environment in which I am not welcome, not wanted, and not protected."

This may be similar to how a person would feel if he discovered he is not welcome at a party to which he thought he was invited. If you were to show up at an invitation-only formal party thinking your name was on the guest list only to discover at the door that your name is not on the list, you may feel quite rejected. In a situation like that you may simply turn around and leave, all the while saying to yourself, "Well, I know where I'm not wanted."

However, a child who shows up in his mother's womb and has a similar experience cannot simply turn around and leave. He has nowhere else to go. The child is forced to remain in this hostile environment, incurring the rejection and disdain of the host every day. This could easily create the feeling of alienation, rejection, and wrongness of being (shame). The child has done nothing wrong. His existence is considered wrong. Thus his very identity is cursed from the womb.

The third significant phrase in Psalm 58:3 is "to go astray." This is the Hebrew word ta'ah. Some of the meanings of this word are "to wander, to vacillate, to reel or stray, to stagger as a drunken man."[11] Thus the result of being estranged in the womb is that in adulthood, one goes astray. If we apply these three expanded definitions to the Scripture passage, the verse would read something like this:

> The man (or woman) who is in a restless, unquiet state, tossed with various evil passions, distracted by many forms of wickedness, and having no peace of conscience, and violent commotion within was alienated, turned aside, treated as an enemy, and made to feel illegitimate or of another family in the womb. These who speak lies

then from the time of birth are made to wander, to vacillate, to reel or stray, to be made to stagger through life
as a drunken man.

Through the years in ministry I have met many people who
seem to have what I call a "Gypsy spirit." No matter where they
are or what they are doing, they are never happy. The grass is
always greener somewhere else. They never feel at home. Thus,
such a person wanders in his Christian life from church to
church. Sometimes he wanders from job to job, city to city, or
even relationship to relationship. When you look at the course
of his life, it is not straight. It is a zigzag pattern with no sta-
bility. This person is literally wandering through life almost as
a drunken man.

When people have been rejected and cursed instead of
blessed in the womb, this often results in a disquieted soul
in childhood and adult life. When the soul has no peace, the
flesh is always busy attempting to bring a false comfort to the
soul through various forms of wickedness, as described above.
Since the soul is never at rest, this person is never at home and
is always looking for something or someone else.

In addition, many negative habits, feelings, and attitudes in
adult life can result directly from estrangement in the womb.
Sometimes these are not serious external sin patterns such
as murder, alcoholism, adultery, or physical violence but are
simply negative habits or emotional response patterns that are
very difficult to change.

When ministering to people in this state, I have sought the
Lord to reveal the root of the behavior, and many times He
has led us to minister to the effects of rejection and cursing in
the womb. Many people have experienced a complete change
in their adult behavior and experience of life after having an
encounter with the Lord at one of our Blessing Generations
Experiences.[12]

One man had struggled all his life with procrastination and being late for appointments. We first prayed and asked the Lord to reveal to this man the root cause of these symptoms. As we waited, he slowly bent over in his chair, then fell down on the floor, curled up in a fetal position and began to quietly weep. When I asked him what he was experiencing, the man said that when we asked the Lord to reveal the root cause of his procrastination, he had an overwhelming feeling of being in his mother's womb and not wanting to be born.

He had heard many angry voices and annoyance from his mother at his existence. In the weeks before his birth, the man's mother and father argued frequently, and there had been several emotional outbursts between them. He was reliving the experience of being warm, secure, and safe in his mother's womb and not wanting to emerge into the hostile environment he heard on the outside.

This man later told us that he had been born more than three weeks after his due date. As we invited the Lord Jesus to minister to him, he felt the Lord remove the deep lie that he would not be wanted or received in any new situation. That lie was replaced with the truth that he would be accepted and welcomed. I could tell that something significant had occurred in this man's life, and he later reported that he no longer struggled with feeling unwanted or not wanting to encounter the unknown. The feelings of fear and torment were simply not there. After that weekend he was rarely late for appointments, and the struggle with procrastination had completely been eliminated. His entire life had been transformed when the Lord replaced the deep emotional lie the man received in the womb with His truth. (See John 8:32.)

Another notable experience demonstrating the power of impartations in the womb occurred during an Ancient Paths Experience several years ago. A Dutch woman said she had a significant bout with serious depression for several weeks at the same time every year. She had consulted several medical professionals and had been combating this depression in prayer for many years, but the depression still returned. Again, we simply asked the Lord to reveal to her the root of her depression. Within seconds she was experiencing an intense feeling of abandonment, loss, and grief. She asked the Lord to show her the origin of this intense emotion. Just then the Holy Spirit showed her that an intense sorrow had come upon her in the womb.

Having been conceived in Holland during the Second World War, she never knew her father. He had gone off to fight with the Dutch army after she was conceived, and unfortunately he was killed in battle and never returned home. In the course of her prayer the woman realized the feeling of intense loss had been imparted to her through her mother when the family received news of her father's death. Through the time of ministry the Lord removed these intense feelings and the lies that attended them, and He replaced them with the impartation of blessing He had wanted her to receive in the womb. Again, this proved to be a life-changing experience for her.

After the time of ministry this woman realized that the time of year she had battled depression was the exact time when news of her father's death had reached her family. Intense feelings of abandonment, loss, grief, and sorrow had so powerfully come upon her mother that they were subsequently imparted to her in the womb. I happened to speak with this woman several years later, and she told me she was completely free of the annual cycle of depression and had never again experienced the same intense emotions since that ministry time.

Years later I discovered Dr. Verny's book, which gave me an even better understanding of how and why an unintentional and unavoidable impartation of negative emotion from a mother to an unborn child could result in a lifelong struggle with depression for the child. Dr. Verny writes:

Some forms of depression can also originate in utero. Usually, these are produced by a major loss. For whatever reason—illness or a distraction—a mother withdraws her love and support from her unborn child; that loss plunges him into a depression. You can see the after-affects of this in an apathetic newborn or a distracted sixteen-year-old; for, like other emotional patterns set in utero, depression may plague a child for the rest of his life.[13]

Other feelings that can be traced back to the cursing of identity in the womb include:

- Rejection
- Depression
- Fear
- Lust
- Anger
- Guilt
- "I'm a mistake."
- "I didn't ask to be born."
- "I don't belong."

The cursing of identity during the time in the womb is not the only cause of these feelings, but it is a major root of many such emotions and negative experiences later in life.

GOD'S PROTECTIVE MEASURES IN ANCIENT HEBREW CULTURE

God was so intent that no one would receive Satan's identity message in the womb that He again placed protective measures in ancient Hebrew culture. God used the same three protective values mentioned in the last chapter to protect a child in the womb. In addition to those three—the Law of Moses and the cultural attitudes toward children and marriage—there was another common practice in biblical Hebrew culture that facilitated the blessing of a child in the womb and protected the child against cursing. It was the practice of relieving an expectant mother of most of her duties during the latter stages of the pregnancy.

In our modern culture the birth of a child is almost a non-event. Many times the mother works up until her water breaks and then rushes to the hospital to have the baby. After a short "maternity leave" the mother is back at work, the baby is off to day care, and life goes on as if nothing has changed.

In contrast, in ancient Hebrew culture the news of a pregnancy was cause for celebration. Because children were considered a gift from God, an expectant mother was treated with special care and honor. First, in general women didn't work outside the home. Caring for her family was considered a high calling. Again, in our modern culture, even in many Christian circles, a woman who is "just a stay-at-home mom" is sometimes seen as not making valuable use of her time and intellect.

Typically in biblical culture, not only was the expectant mother at home, but also during the last one or even two trimesters her extended family would do much of her household work. The expectant mother was encouraged to spend her time praying, caring for her herself and the unborn child, and preparing herself for the birth. In the Hebrew family the unborn child was a high priority to both the mother and the family in general. This protective measure established by God created the maximum opportunity for an unborn child to receive regular impartation of blessing while in the womb. Again, it is important for us today to reestablish in our communities a culture of blessing that facilitates this same blessing of children in the womb.

••• BLESSING TOOLBOX •••

Let's now look at specific prayers to pray over children in the womb. Again, if father and mother are both available, I encourage you to pray any of the pertinent prayers together as a couple. If only one parent is available, then pray individually. All the prayers below are samples that you can use to create your own personalized prayers and blessings to speak over your child. You don't have to use these exact words; they are written simply to be a starting point for you.

REMEDIAL PRAYERS TO BREAK THE CURSE

If you tried to abort your child

Attempting to abort a child in the womb, of course, is one of the most powerful ways of imparting Satan's identity message. This is the bad news. The good news is that Jesus Christ died and shed His blood to forgive you of your sin and to heal, restore, and bless the identity of your child. If you attempted to abort your child, I encourage you to follow the steps below.

1. Renounce and repent of the sin of attempted murder and receive forgiveness.

Father, I recognize today that I sinned against You and against my son/daughter by attempting to abort my child. I acknowledge that abortion is murder, so I acknowledge that I attempted to commit murder. Lord, I renounce the sin of attempted murder, and I repent of it and turn completely away from it. I can't pay for this sin, but I recognize that Jesus Christ died to pay for my sin. Today I receive the blood of Jesus to pay for the attempted murder of my child, and because Jesus paid for this sin, today I receive Your forgiveness. Father, because You have forgiven me, today I forgive myself for the sin of attempted murder.

2. Pray blessing over the life of your child.

Father, we now bless [your child's name] *in the mighty name of Jesus Christ with life, health, and peace. We declare over* [your child's name] *that he/ she is wanted, accepted, and safe here in our family. You gave him/her to us, and today we receive* [your child's name] *as the precious gift he/she is to us.*

[Your child's name], *we bless the time you spent in your mother's womb. By the blood of Jesus Christ we break the power of every message the enemy tried to send to you. We declare over you that you were conceived by the will of God right on time. We bless the day of your conception and every day you spent in the womb until the day you were born. God kept you safe in your mother's womb, and you were born right on time. You are our child, and we love you. We receive your life as a unique gift from God to our family, and we thank God for making you a part of our family in His unique and special timing. You are absolutely unique, and no one else can accomplish or fulfill your purpose on earth. We bless your life, your spirit, your health, your destiny and purpose, and your place in our family. May you be blessed in all you are and all you do all the days of your life.*

If you considered your child an intrusion into your life or cursed your child's identity while he/she was in the womb

1. Renounce and repent of inadvertently or intentionally cursing the identity of your child and receive forgiveness.

Father, I recognize today that I was the devil's agent to send to my child a wrong identity message. Lord, I renounce the sin of cursing my child's identity, and I

*repent of it and turn completely away from it. I can't
pay for this, but I recognize that Jesus Christ died
to pay for my sin. Today I receive the blood of Jesus to
pay for my cursing my child's identity, and because
Jesus Christ paid for this sin, today I receive Your forgiveness. Father, because You have forgiven me, today
I forgive myself for cursing the identity of my child.*

2. Pray blessing over the life of your child.

I suggest you pray the same prayer of blessing over your
child included above.

If you never knew to pray blessing over your child during his time in the womb

If you did not realize the value of blessing your child in the
womb, I suggest that you now pray over your child the same
prayer of blessing included above.

PREVENTATIVE PRAYERS TO RELEASE THE BLESSING

Now that you understand God's intent for every child to be
blessed in the womb, start today blessing any children or
grandchildren God gives you each day while they are growing
in the womb. Pray for the child and speak words of love, welcome, and blessing. I suggest you pray something like this:

Father God, thank You for [your child's name]. *He
is a precious gift to us. We pray that you keep
him strong and healthy and full of life in the
womb. Lord, fill* [your child's name] *even now
in the womb with Your Holy Spirit and let him
feel Your love and protection today in the womb.*

Hello, little one, this is your father/mother [or
grandmother/grandfather]. *I love you. I can't wait to
see you when you are born and to kiss your precious
little face. We are so glad you are here, and we will*

always be here for you, take care of you, and keep you safe. You belong in this family, and you have a place here with us. You were fearfully and wonderfully made by God, and He has set you apart even from your mother's womb to serve the Lord Jesus Christ all the days of your life. I declare this day that your life is completely off limits to Satan and all demonic spirits. We declare that you are dedicated in every aspect of your life to the Lord Jesus Christ and to His plan and purpose for you today and all the days of your life.

You are a blessing to everyone you meet, and you can expect to have God's favor on your life everywhere you go. You are absolutely unique, and no one else can be who God has created you to be or do what God has gifted you to do. I want you to know that you will always be safe and welcome here. There is nothing that you can ever do that will cause us to reject or abandon you. I bless your spirit today with the life of God. I bless your mind with intelligence and wisdom. I bless your emotions with enthusiasm, security, and peace. I bless your body with physical health and life. May you grow and develop in every aspect—spirit, soul, and body—into the person God has planned for you to be. May you abide in God's love and peace this day, in Jesus's name, amen.

Chapter 6

BLESSING YOUR CHILD
AT BIRTH

I BELIEVE THERE IS a party in heaven each time a child is born. Angels rejoice, and the Father looks at the new little person He has made and declares something much like what He said in Genesis after each step of creation: *It is very good* (Gen. 1:31). God was delighted in you at your birth, and He has delighted in each child born into your family.

KEY ROLE PLAYER

Both parents play a key role in imparting a message to the heart of the child at the time of birth. God intends to use both father and mother to impart love and acceptance of the child's personhood and gender. Yet, again, while the father is very important to impart blessing, it is primarily the mother who will answer the key question in the child's heart.

KEY QUESTION TO BE ANSWERED

The key questions that either God or Satan will answer through the agency of parents are: *Am I what you expected and wanted? Am I OK, or is something wrong with me? Will anyone take care of me?*

Probably none of us can remember being born, but I'm sure it must be a very scary experience for a baby. Moving from the warm, protected environment in the womb, where all the child's needs are met, to a cold, noisy, unprotected environment could be very terrifying. That's why the immediate question in the heart of the child would be, "Who will take care of me?"

No one ever brought a baby home from the hospital and said, "Welcome to your new home. Here is your room. The bathroom is just down the hall. Farther down is the kitchen. Help yourself to anything you want. We're so glad you're here. Make yourself at home." A baby is completely helpless. He cannot meet any of his own needs, and without help he will die. So once the birth has taken place, that newborn needs to know whether his needs will continue to be met even though he is no longer protected and automatically cared for as he was in the womb.

Of course, the devil would like to tell the child, "You are all alone now without anyone who loves you or cares for you. There is something wrong with you, and consequently no one wants you, and no one will take care of you. You must fend for yourself, and since you can't, you will die."

God, on the other hand, intends to use the parents to send exactly the opposite message. His message is: "Welcome! You are supposed to be here. You are a gift from God to us. We've been waiting to see you face-to-face, and you are even more wonderful and beautiful than we had imagined. You are exactly who we wanted. You are just perfect! We are here to meet your every need. There's no need to fear or worry about anything. You can just kick back and relax. Now is the only time in your life when you will have no responsibilities and no burdens or pressures. Others will wait on you hand and foot and meet your every need. One specific agent of God, your mom, will make you and your needs top priority in her schedule. We love and bless you, and we welcome you into our family."

BLESSING AND CURSING
AT THE TIME OF BIRTH

It was the Father's intent for each child to receive his parents' blessing right at the time of birth. I believe God intended for there to be one clear message from the heart of the Father through the parents to the heart of the child. However, if the parents feel disappointment, fear, stress, or trauma, the message they send may be something other than the one from the heart of God. So what might blessing and cursing look like at the time of birth?

Blessing at the time of birth may involve:

1. Ensuring the child receives verbal and physical communication from the parents that he is wanted, accepted, and welcome, and the mother providing love and physical nurture

2. The parents receiving the child as the sex God created him to be

3. The parents imparting a name with spiritual meaning and having a time of spiritual impartation to the child soon after birth

4. A reasonably trauma-free birth

Cursing at the time of birth may include:

1. The parents communicating to the child verbally and physically that he is not wanted and not welcome. The baby is not loved, held, cuddled, or physically nurtured by his mother.

2. The parents expressing disappointment in the child's gender and not receiving the child as the sex God created him to be

3. The parents giving the child a demeaning or negative name, and having no time of spiritual impartation, or worse yet, spiritually dedicating the child to Satan, idolatrous gods, or demonic spirits

4. The child experiencing significant physical trauma at birth

Consequences of Blessing and Cursing at Birth

When a baby is held, accepted, and nurtured at the time of birth, he tends to develop a strong sense of security and emotional peace. God is able to use that child's parents to impart a consistent message into the child's heart regarding his identity and destiny. On the other hand, when a baby is rejected, not held, and not nurtured, the child can develop feelings of insecurity and a fear of death right from the beginning.

Teams from our ministry have prayed for people who have had great difficulty trusting God in difficult circumstances or trusting a spouse or others close to them. When we have asked the Lord to reveal the source of the insecurity and inability to trust, the person has often been led back to a sense of rejection at the time of birth. This has also resulted in a need to control everything that happens in their lives.

A deep-seated lie rooted in fear is established in the heart from birth that says, "No one really loves me and will meet my needs. Therefore I can trust no one and must put a shell around my heart and do my best to meet all my own needs." This person may then strive to meet his own needs for the rest of his life.

A second consequence that may come from rejection at birth is an undue drive to perform in order to obtain acceptance. The lie imparted is: "I obviously have no inherent value. Therefore I must do something outstanding to gain the acceptance and approval of those important to me." This person may strive all his life to become "somebody" because deep inside he feels like a "nobody."

GENDER BLESSING OR CURSING AT BIRTH

I mentioned that one way an infant may be blessed or cursed at birth is through the parents' acceptance or rejection of his gender. When parents affirm a baby as the boy or girl God created, this again establishes deep inside a self-acceptance and settled sense of gender identity. This person goes through life looking in the mirror and taking pleasure in his gender; he believes God did a good job when He created him. A person blessed at birth is seldom confused about gender roles later in life and rarely deals with same-sex attraction.

On the other hand, a person whose gender identity was rejected at birth may constantly struggle with the feeling that God played a cruel joke when He established his gender. These individuals may even feel they were born the wrong sex. Now, obviously, God doesn't put anyone in the wrong body, but many people have parents who make them think something is wrong with their gender.

With ultrasound technology people can know a baby's gender long before birth. Parents who desperately wanted a girl, for instance, may experience disappointment at the fact that they are having a boy, and that disappointment may be expressed to the child consciously or unconsciously. Some parents may go so far as to give the boy a masculine form of the chosen girl's name, calling their son Ashton, for instance, instead of Ashley.

When this kind of thing happens, right at birth the child receives an impartation to his heart that says, "You're not what we want. You're not what we expected. Something is wrong with you!" This little boy may come to believe, "I can't ever meet the expectations of my parents, because I'm the wrong sex. It's not possible for me to be who I'm supposed to be." This is a lie, but the child gets confused by the competing messages he hears—the one God is speaking to him versus the one Satan is sending through his parents.

As I have ministered to people through the years, I have found that little girls tend to respond in one of two ways to their parents rejecting their gender at birth. Some work to become the boy her father wanted. As she grows, she becomes a tomboy and takes an interest in the things she thinks will please her dad. This is not the reason all girls enjoy male-oriented activities, but I have found that this is most often the case.

The interesting thing is that often this behavior does please the father. Dad loves taking her fishing, to baseball games, and doing the other activities he dreamed of enjoying with a son. Consequently in her heart this little girl takes on an identity of being "just one of the guys," and she receives significant affirmation and blessing from her father in the early years of life.

Yet when she reaches puberty, it becomes clear that she is not one of the guys. In his attempt to affirm her as a young woman, Dad no longer wrestles with her or conveys the same kind of physical affection he once did. This withdrawal can easily be perceived as more rejection, and the daughter can begin to believe the devil's lie that her gender is "wrong."

One woman I met had always despised being a woman, and consequently as an adult she dressed in clothing designed to hide her femininity. She was actually a very beautiful woman, but she didn't want anyone to know that. As we prayed, the Lord revealed that this tendency was a result of her father rejecting her gender at birth. I am convinced that God never intended for any woman to feel this way about herself. God wants every woman to love being a woman, to know God did a great job when He made her. Yet I encounter many women who have embraced the enemy's lie and feel deep down that they were cheated because they weren't created male.

The second thing that can happen to girls who are not blessed at birth is that they can develop a compulsion to achieve. Since the enemy used her parents to impart his lie, she begins to feel that she has no inherent worth, so she must strive to do something great to gain acceptance and approval. She thinks she must have a successful career, make a lot of money, excel at sports—anything to feel valuable.

This leads to a lifelong battle with performance orientation and deep frustration. Because the lie inside keeps the soul continually out of peace, she can never accomplish enough to dispel the deep feeling of inner worthlessness. Fortunately we have seen many women whose femininity was cursed at birth totally set free when we led them through a process that allowed the Lord to remove the deep-rooted identity lie and replace it with His truth. (See John 8:32.)

The same things that happen to girls can occur in boys. The boy rejected at birth by his parents may strive to earn value by becoming wealthy, powerful, famous, or all three. Or he may attempt to become the little girl his parents wanted. I have often seen a father's gender rejection at birth become the seedbed of homosexuality in a son's heart. Knowing his father is disappointed with his gender, boys as young as three, four, or five years old will show interest in dolls, fashion, and other more feminine activities.

The son wants to please his dad, but this behavior probably won't do the trick. Dad will likely reject the little boy and possibly even make cruel comments or convey his displeasure nonverbally. This may be confusing for the son, since he was only trying to be the little girl his father seemed to want. The enemy may then deepen the lie by saying it's not only his gender that displeases his father but his entire being, that there is just something inherently inadequate and displeasing with him as a person.

If this scenario unfolds this way and the father further rejects the son, the mom will probably try to comfort and shelter her son. She'll gather her little boy in her arms and say, "Honey, I love you. Your dad does too; he just doesn't know how to show it. There's nothing wrong with you. You're special. You're precious. I love you."

Now, which one of these two people do you think this little boy will want to open up to and be around? Harsh, ridiculing Dad or kind, compassionate Mom? Probably Mom. Over time this little boy will spend more time around women and become more effeminate. Dad will only have a harder time relating to him. But Dad has another opportunity right at puberty to affirm his son's masculinity and release him into his adult identity as a man. (We will discuss this more fully in a later chapter.) However, if Dad doesn't know how to bless his son at puberty and instead imparts further rejection, then there's a strong possibility that this son will be drawn into a homosexual lifestyle in his early teenage years.

Having been denied all his life gender affirmation and his father's blessing, the young man, now in his teenage years, will search for this approval elsewhere. Sadly this affirmation will likely come from a man who is himself bound in a homosexual lifestyle. He will tell the son what the boy longed to hear from his father: "I love you. I value you. I'm proud of you. You are special. You're wonderful. You're handsome. You're a great man. You're a wonderful person." This may not begin as a sexual relationship, but it often devolves into one. This is not the only way young men enter a gay lifestyle, but I have seen this scenario many times in ministry.

How does this young man's father respond? He will probably heap on more ridicule and rejection. The irony is that the father held the key to influence his son's identity and destiny all along, but instead of affirming the gender God gave his child, the father planted a seed of gender rejection and homosexuality in his son at birth. He then watered that seed and continued to fertilize it by not blessing his son throughout his childhood.

Fortunately it is possible for the Lord Jesus to remove this deep identity lie from the hearts of sons and replace it with the truth that should have been imparted through a human father. Many times our ministry teams have seen the Lord resolve this situation in families who have participated in a Blessing Generations Experience.

WHAT'S IN A NAME?

A third way children can be blessed or cursed at the time of birth is through the impartation of a meaningful name. A good name will contain character qualities and hint at the child's destiny. In Hebrew culture there is traditionally a ceremony eight days after a child's birth during which the parents, after seeking the Lord, impart a meaningful name to the child.

There is a Hebrew saying that goes, "You can't really know a man until you know his name." Why? Because his name contains his character and sometimes a job description. Wouldn't it be amazing if you received your adult job description eight days after birth? This is how it was for many people we encounter in the Bible. In contrast, I encounter many Christians who are not certain what they are supposed to do with their lives even at age forty, fifty, or sixty.

Many times we do not know what the names we use in Western culture even mean. Bob, Sue, and Sam have rich meaning in their original languages, but too often parents choose these names without knowing what that meaning is.

It is interesting to note that in the Book of Daniel the first thing the Babylonian king Nebuchadnezzar wanted to do when he inducted the four Hebrew young men into his service was to change their names. Their Hebrew names directly connected them to the service of Yahweh, the God of Israel. The king wanted to break that connection and link them by name to the service of his idolatrous gods.

Daniel in Hebrew means "Yahweh is my lawgiver or judge." The king changed his name to Belteshazzar, which means "the one who serves Baal." Likewise the names of the other three Hebrew men were changed to break their allegiance to Yahweh and establish their service to Babylonian gods.

Something similar happened to the last son Jacob had with his wife, Rachel. She died in childbirth, but before she passed away, she named her son Ben-oni, which means "son of my sorrow." After her death Jacob renamed his son Benjamin, which means "son of my right hand." Jacob changed his son's name from a curse to a blessing. He said in essence, "You are not a son of sorrow. This is not what you shall be known for. You are the son of my right hand."

The name Jesus in Hebrew is Yeshua. This name actually means, "The Lord [Yahweh] is salvation." This name is quite descriptive of Jesus's assignment as an adult—He came to bring the Lord's salvation to all mankind. His job description was in His name.

One last potent example is that of Elijah. This name means "Yahweh is God." In Elijah's day Israel had been at war with a land to the north called Phoenicia. To finally reach a peace accord, they agreed to marry each other's royalty. So the king of Phoenicia, a man named Eth-baal, made the deal with Ahab, the king of Israel. As you may have figured out, Eth-baal means "servant of Baal."

Eth-baal had a daughter named Jezebel. She also served Baal, the god of her father, and when she became Israel's queen, she had one primary purpose in her mind: to turn the nation of Israel from worshipping Yahweh to worshipping Baal. So the message Jezebel continually promoted throughout the land was "Baal is God."

This is the situation Elijah faced. Fortunately his parents sought the Lord to discover what they should name him, and God told them to give him the name Elijah, which means "Yahweh is God." When Elijah became a prophet in adulthood, his prophetic message was "Yahweh is God." His job was to proclaim his name throughout the land and turn the nation back to Yahweh.

To Jezebel, Elijah's very name was an affront. Every time the name Elijah was spoken, it was a declaration that Baal is not God, but Yahweh is God. Even when Elijah was a little boy, every time his parents called his name, they were burning into his young soul his prophetic calling. Is it any wonder that in his early adulthood Elijah stood on Mount Carmel and confronted the prophets of Baal about the identity of the one true God? He slew 450 prophets of Baal and 400 prophets of the Asherah while proclaiming his message, which simply was his name (1 Kings 18). I believe the confidence to single-handedly defeat the prophets of Baal and turn the nation of Israel back to Yahweh was in the blessing imparted to Elijah in his name at birth.

On the other hand there are many today whose parents arbitrarily choose names for them. I remember hearing about a neighbor boy who loved our family dog so much he gave his firstborn daughter the same name. There was nothing wrong with the name itself, but what a heritage to give a child! Can you imagine ever trying to explain to your daughter that she was named after a dog you knew while growing up?

POTENTIAL CURSING
THROUGH BIRTH TRAUMA

A fourth way the identity of a child may be cursed or blessed at birth is through physical trauma or the lack thereof. In general, a child is blessed when the birth is uneventful and trauma-free. This protects the child from growing up with irrational fears and phobias.

Certainly no mother plans for trauma during birth. Yet I mention this because sometimes fears, phobias, and compulsions are rooted in traumatic birth experiences. I have ministered to various people who have struggled with an irrational fear of choking on food or being in tight, restricted places. When we have asked the Lord to expose the time or events through which the deep emotional lie was imparted, many times He has shown us that the enemy took advantage of birth trauma to impart an irrational fear.

The Bible tells us in Hebrews 2:14–15 that the devil uses the "fear of death" to keep people subject to slavery (bondage) all the days of their lives. Thus many compulsive habits and bondages found in adulthood are rooted in a deep fear of death established at birth. Some of the results of a fear of death imparted at birth include fear of choking, fear of flying, irrational fear of being killed, inability to properly bond with mother, learning difficulties, and craving for physical contact.

GOD'S PROTECTIVE MEASURES IN ANCIENT HEBREW CULTURE

I have observed three protective customs that God established in ancient Hebrew culture to ensure children received His message of identity and destiny at the time of birth.

1. The entire community and extended family anticipated the birth of the child with joy and made the birth a priority.

2. The family and entire community held a celebration in honor of the child's arrival on the eighth day after birth. At this time both the rabbi and

the parents imparted a spiritual blessing to the child.

3. The parents sought the Lord for a meaningful name imbedded with the child's identity and destiny, and they imparted that name to the child at the celebration.

The birth of a child in ancient Hebrew culture was considered a major event. On the eighth day there would be a blessing imparted by both the parents and a spiritual authority. The rabbi would come and bless the child. If the infant were a boy, the covenant of Abraham would be established through circumcision. That boy would then bear a physical mark in his body that declares, "You are not like everybody else. There's something unique about you, something special. You are a Jew. You are inextricably connected by covenant to the God of Abraham, Isaac, and Jacob—and don't you ever forget it! Don't you ever live like those who have no covenant!"

If the child were a girl, there was no circumcision, but still a party was given to welcome the new family member. A name would still be imparted and a prophetic blessing pronounced over her. Since everyone considered children a blessing from the Lord, they stopped what they were doing to celebrate the arrival of the new family member on the eighth day. I've always thought of this sort of as God's "Welcome Wagon."

In contrast, many parents today don't recognize their responsibility to bless, dedicate to God, and impart a meaningful name to their child. They simply take the child to a priest, pastor, or rabbi and leave it to the clergy to dedicate the child to God. Unfortunately the pastor will not stand before God to account for the impartation of identity and destiny to your child. You the parent will. The pastor's job is to equip the saints for the work of service, not to do the work of service for them (Eph. 4:11–13).

In ancient Hebrew culture there was almost no chance that a child would not be blessed at birth. How different is our culture today! The chances that a child would not be blessed at birth is significant since we don't have the same protective measures that God placed in Hebrew culture to ensure that every child would be blessed at birth.

••• BLESSING TOOLBOX •••

This Blessing Toolbox includes remedial prayers to pray in the event that you did not bless your children at birth and prayers you can pray to reverse the cursing of identity and release the blessing. We will then look at specific prayers you can pray at the birth of your child. Either one or both parents can pray these prayers. If you are the only parent who is willing or available to pray for your child, rest assured that you have the spiritual authority to pray these prayers over your children. As in previous chapters, these prayers are to serve as a guide; feel free to modify or personalize them to fit your family and situation.

REMEDIAL PRAYERS TO BREAK THE CURSE

If you conveyed disappointment at birth over your child's gender

1. Repent before God (not in your child's presence) of not accepting His choice of your child's gender.

Father, I recognize today that I am not God and You are. I very much wanted a boy/girl, and You created [your child's name] to be a girl/boy. Please forgive me for rejecting Your choice of my child's gender. Today I renounce the disappointment I expressed over my child's gender, and I fully accept [your child's name] *as the wonderful little boy/girl You created him/her to be. In the name of Jesus I break the power of any curse I released over* [your child's name]*'s gender identity as a boy/girl, and I declare that the blood of Jesus Christ is sufficient to remove any gender identity curse I released in* [your child's name]*'s life. I ask You this day to dig up and remove any seed of homosexuality that I may have unknowingly planted in* [your child's name]*'s heart at birth and replace it with the seed of Your identity truth. I now fully release the blessing that Jesus Christ died to pay for to* [your child's name], *and I bless his/her identity as a boy/girl.*

2. Pray a blessing (in your child's presence) over your child's gender identity.

Father, we now bless [your child's name] *and thank You that You created him/her as a precious little boy/ girl. We fully accept and bless* [your child's name] *as the boy/girl You created him/her to be. In the name of Jesus we bless* [your child's name]*'s identity. We declare this day that* [your child's name] *will grow to be a man/woman of God who will serve the Lord Jesus all the days of his/her life.*

If your child experienced excessive trauma during birth

Pray to break the power of the fear of death and all other fears or disquietedness of soul over your son/daughter, and release blessing upon your child's life.

Father, in the name of Jesus, we break the power of the fear of death over [your child's name]. *We declare that he/she shall live and not die. Jesus Christ died and shed His blood that* [your child's name] *might live and fulfill his/her destiny on the earth. We cancel every plan of Satan for our child and place his/her life and destiny in God's hands. Lord God, we now release Your supernatural peace that passes all understanding to* [your child's name]*'s inner man and a supernatural sense of security, knowing that You have appointed his/her days on the earth. We bless* [your child's name]*'s life and his/her birth and declare that* [your child's name] *shall dwell in peace and security all the days of his/her life, in Jesus's name, amen.*

If you rejected your child at birth

1. Repent before God (not in your child's presence) of rejecting your child.

Father, this day we acknowledge that we were selfish and rejected [your child's name] *at the time of his/her birth. That was wrong and contrary to the message You wanted us to convey to our son/daughter. Father, please forgive us in the name of Jesus Christ. Today we renounce the disappointment and rejection we expressed to our child at birth, and we fully accept* [your child's name] *as a gift from You to our family. In the name of Jesus we break the power of any curse of rejection we released over* [your child's name]*'s identity, and we declare that the blood of Jesus Christ is sufficient to remove any gender identity curse we released in our child's life. We now fully release the blessing to our child that Jesus Christ died to secure, and I bless his/her birth and declare that my child shall prosper in all areas of life from this day forward.*

2. Pray over your child (in your child's presence) to release your acceptance and blessing to your child.

Father, we now bless [your child's name] *and thank You that You created him/her as a precious little boy/girl. We fully accept and bless* [your child's name]*'s birth and life. In the name of Jesus we bless* [your child's name]*'s identity as a boy/girl. We declare this day,* [your child's name], *that you are loved and welcome. You belong in our family. We receive you as the precious gift that you are to our family, and we declare that you will prosper in your life and grow to be a man/woman of God who will serve the Lord Jesus Christ all his/her life.*

If you as a mother had an inordinate fear of delivery that you know imparted fear or insecurity into the heart of your child

Pray to renounce the fear and break its power over your child's life; then release blessing upon your child.

Father, in the name of Jesus I renounce the fear I embraced before and during the delivery of my baby. Forgive me for not fully trusting You in the birth process. Today I cancel the curse of fear that I released into [your child's name]*'s life, and I break the power of fear over my child's mind, emotions, and body. I declare that my child shall live and not die. Jesus Christ died and shed His blood that* [your child's name] *might live and fulfill his/her destiny on the earth. I cancel every plan of Satan for my child and place his/her life and destiny in God's hands. Lord God, I now release Your supernatural peace that passes all understanding to* [your child's name]*'s inner man and a supernatural sense of security to know that You have appointed his/her days on the earth. I bless* [your child's name] *and his/her birth and declare that* [your child's name] *shall dwell in peace and security all the days of his/her life, in Jesus's name, amen.*

If your child was born after you lost one or more babies before birth

Pray over your child to break the power of feeling like a replacement for someone else and any pressure to fulfill another person's purpose and destiny.

Father, we declare this day that [your child's name] *is not a replacement for anyone. My child is a unique individual You created to fulfill a unique and specific destiny and purpose. Today we relinquish any expectation we placed upon* [your child's name] *other than to be exactly who You created him/her to be. In the name of Jesus we break any spiritual or soul connection we created between* [your child's name] *and the child we lost, and we fully release* [your child's name] *to be himself/herself and to grow as the individual God created him/her to be.* [Your child's name], *we bless you to be yourself and to fulfill the purpose and destiny God has for you. We love you, accept you, and declare that you are welcome and belong in our family as the person God made you.*

PRAYERS TO RELEASE THE BLESSING

Conduct a formal ceremony of blessing roughly eight days after your child's birth.

At that ceremony confirm the child's value, gender identity, and destiny; give him/her a meaningful name; and dedicate the baby to God. As I mentioned earlier, the role of the pastor or congregational leader is to help train and equip the parents to impart blessing to their children, not to do it for them. While the pastor may also pray over the baby, it is the responsibility of the parents to pray in advance and prepare to impart blessing and destiny into the lives of their children shortly after birth. With such understanding the parents may wish to pray something similar to the following:

> *Father, this day we thank You for creating* [your child's name] *and placing him/her in our family. Today we declare over you,* [your child's name], *that you are welcome and belong in our family. We will never abandon or forsake you. You will always be our child, and we will love and pray for you all the days of your life.*
>
> *We named you* [your child's name] *because it means* [state the meaning], *and God showed us that you would be* [state any character qualities and/or destiny God revealed to you about your child]. *The Lord also showed us* [state any other prophetic words, revelations, or visions God has given you regarding your child]. *Key Scripture verses that the Lord gave us for you are:* [state any key Scripture verses that the Lord gave you to pray over your son/daughter].
>
> *We declare that you,* [your child's name], *are blessed and will always be highly favored by God and by men. You are not an ordinary child, but you have been brought into a family connected by covenant to the God of Abraham, Isaac, and Jacob. As such you can expect to be blessed and prosper all the days of your life.* [Your child's name], *this day*

*we dedicate you to the Lord Jesus Christ to worship
and serve Him all the days of your life. Amen!*

Speak words of love, acceptance, welcome, and affirmation of gender identity at birth, and commit to meet all your child's needs.

Father God, thank You for [your child's name]. *He/
she is a precious gift to us. We bless him/her on this
special day. We pray that you keep our child strong
and healthy as he/she grows. Lord, again fill* [your
child's name] *even now in the first few minutes after
birth with Your Holy Spirit, and let him/her feel
Your love and protection today.*

*Hello, little one, this is your mom and dad. We
love you. We have been waiting to see you face-to-
face, and now we do. You are a beautiful little boy/
girl. You are exactly who we wanted you to be. God
did a wonderful thing by making you a boy/girl. We
are so delighted in who God made you. Today we
celebrate your birth with the angels in heaven and
declare that you are welcome in this world and in
our family. We have been expecting you and have
made a place for you. We are so glad you are here,
and we will always be here for you, take care of you,
and keep you safe. We will see that every need you
have is met.*

*You were fearfully and wonderfully made by God,
and He has set you apart even from your mother's
womb to serve the Lord Jesus Christ all the days of
your life. We declare this day that your life is completely off-limits to Satan and all demonic spirits.
We declare that you are dedicated in every aspect of
your life to the Lord Jesus Christ and to His plan and
purpose for you today and all the days of your life.*

You are a blessing to all you meet, and you can expect to have God's favor on your life everywhere you go. You are absolutely unique, and no one else can be who God has created you to be or do what God has gifted you to do. We want you to know that you will always be safe and welcome here. There is nothing that you can ever do to cause us to reject or abandon you.

We bless your spirit today with the life of God. We bless your mind with intelligence and wisdom. We bless your emotions with enthusiasm, security, and peace. We bless your body with physical health and strength. May you grow and develop in every aspect—spirit, soul, and body—into the person God has planned for you to be. May you abide in God's love and peace this day, in Jesus's name, amen.

Chapter 7

BLESSING YOUR CHILD IN INFANCY AND EARLY CHILDHOOD

A NOTHER KEY TIME at which blessing or cursing can occur is during infancy and early childhood. A child is very vulnerable at this stage because he cannot meet any of his own needs. If he doesn't feel secure that his needs will be met, the child may begin to trust no one but himself. Of course, this is not a moment in time but a season of life during which the child is looking for consistent nurture and care. It is this consistency that allows a child to learn to trust others.

KEY ROLE PLAYER

The key roll player in blessing a child in infancy and early childhood is the mother. While the affection of the father is important, it is really the mother's care that is critical to establishing basic trust during this key time of life. She is the one who can answer the key question in the child's heart with the divine truth that will bring peace to her child's soul.

KEY QUESTION TO BE ANSWERED

In early childhood the key questions to be answered are: *Is there anyone I can really trust to meet my needs? Is there anyone here bigger, stronger, and wiser than I am, who truly loves and cares about me?*

An infant must trust people outside himself to survive. As a result, the enemy wants to make sure the child receives no consistent care, thus creating a significant fear of death, inner turmoil, and a struggle to survive. The enemy wants the child to think, "If there is nobody I can count on to meet my needs, then I'll have to meet all my own needs." If this is not possible for the infant or toddler to accomplish, and it likely will not be, he will experience much fear, and his soul will not be at rest.

BLESSING AND CURSING IN INFANCY AND EARLY CHILDHOOD

Of course it was God's plan for children to receive a powerful message of blessing through their parents in infancy and throughout early childhood. Below are some of the ways parents can either bless or curse their children in this phase of development.

Blessing at the time of infancy may include:

1. The parents communicating verbally and physically that the child is wanted, accepted, received, and welcome, with the mother in particular loving, holding, and physically nurturing the baby

2. The mother breast-feeding the infant to help create a physical and emotional bond

3. The mother giving consistent care and meeting the child's physical and emotional needs, thus encouraging him to trust someone outside himself to meet his needs

4. The father expressing significant amounts of physical touch and affection

Cursing at the time of infancy may include:

1. The parents communicating verbally and physically that the child is not wanted and not welcome,

and the mother withholding love, affection, or physical nurture

2. The mother not creating a physical or emotional bond through breast-feeding or other forms of meaningful touch and nurturing

3. The child receiving inconsistent care because Mom is not steadily available to meet his physical and emotional needs and therefore outsources this responsibility to an array of caregivers (relatives, day-care workers, nannies, etc.)

4. The father not showing appropriate physical touch and affection

POTENTIAL CONSEQUENCES OF BLESSING AND CURSING IN EARLY CHILDHOOD

Children need lots of physical touch and affection from their parents. Cuddling and other forms of physical touch create healthy bonding and impart a sense of security, which is part of the blessing God intended. Research scientist James Prescott, PhD, who has studied the effects of early childhood sensory deprivation, says, "If you don't bond with anyone as a child, you're not going to bond with anyone as an adult."[1]

Women's bodies have the natural capacity to nourish their babies. This is part of God's design to bless children. Breast-feeding ensures an infant receives lots of physical touch and nurturing. The baby naturally bonds with his mother as he is held and cuddled several times per day. In ancient Hebrew culture (and in most past cultures) it was typical for a mother to breast-feed her children. In our modern Western culture many people prefer to bottle-feed their babies. One common reason is that many mothers work outside the home and are not available to breast-feed several times a day.

Through my years of ministry I have found that many people who did not receive blessing through a mother's touch during infancy develop a deep inner craving for physical touch and tactile stimulation later in life. This need for physical touch and affection is sometimes sexualized. I have encountered many men who looked to satisfy this inner need for touch through physical intimacy with their wives. However, this is not what marital intimacy was created to do.

Many times when I've counseled couples, the wives have told me privately that they feel overwhelmed by their husbands' needs. "Pastor," they say, "I enjoy sexual intimacy as much as anyone, but my husband's need is excessive. I am becoming exhausted." As I have prayed with the husbands to discover the root issue, the Lord has exposed that there is a deep need for nurture in the heart of a little boy who was never cuddled as an infant.

Young children who have not experienced physical love and cuddling from their parents will frequently develop doubt that their needs will be met. When this happens, the enemy often attempts to impart a fear of death in the infant, who has no ability to care for himself. If there is not consistent cuddling and nurturing from Mom, the child may from an early age begin to trust in himself to meet his own needs, fearing he will die otherwise. The child does not usually do this consciously. He simply begins to conclude, "No one is here to meet my needs, so I had better take care of myself. Since no one is here for me, I won't trust anyone outside myself to provide for me."

When this fear and insecurity are established deep inside a child, they do not lessen as he grows and enters adulthood. They simply produce a teenager or adult with an inability to trust his friends, spouse, or even God. As an adult, this person may give his life to Christ and say, "Lord, I trust You with my whole life." Yet when crisis awakens the deep fear inside, this person will immediately take his life out of God's hands and act on his own behalf.

We have prayed for several people who have had a deep inability to trust a spouse or God. When we asked the Holy Spirit when this insecurity started, we quickly learn that it started in infancy due to a lack of nurturing. The first time I encountered this in a married man, I wasn't sure how to help him. So we prayed and asked God how to meet his deep need for nurture since he could not now receive it from his mother. The Lord instructed me to tell this man that God was the only one who could meet his need.

In this particular case the Holy Spirit reminded the husband that one of God's Hebrew names is *El Shaddai*. The traditional meaning of the name is "the one who is more than enough to meet any need." The literal meaning is "the double-breasted one." Thus El Shaddai, who created man in His own image, male and female, is the double-breasted one who is more than enough to minister to the love deficiency in the heart of any man.

As I shared this with this man and asked him to open his heart to El Shaddai, God began to minister to the depths of his heart and fill him with the love and security that should have been imparted in infancy. After allowing the Holy Spirit to do a deep work in his heart, the man reported that his need for physical intimacy had been quieted, and both he and his wife were now very satisfied with their sexual relationship.

Since I ministered to that couple, I have encountered this situation many times at our Blessing Generations weekend events. I praise God that others have experienced a similar heart resolution when they received from God the impartation of blessing they were supposed to get from their mothers in infancy.

In Hebrew culture it was typical for a mother to be available to cuddle, hold, and meet the needs of her small children. She was neither working outside the home nor involved in twenty-five other activities as many mothers today are. A mother's role was held in high esteem. There was very little chance that a child in that culture would not be cuddled, breast-fed, and nurtured because this was a mother's top priority, and it is what society expected of her.

In contrast, I believe motherhood has been significantly devalued in our culture today. A stay-at-home mom is sometimes thought to be lazy or unproductive. Even among Christians there is an expectation that a woman should earn money, have a career, or be involved in ministry outside the home. Sadly in our culture there is a significant chance that a child could pass through early childhood without much cuddling and blessing through physical touch.

In reality, motherhood is a very high calling in the sight of God. Nurturing and sowing into the lives of her children is one of the most important things a mother will do. I believe it should be the exception, not the norm, for a mother to work outside the home. I realize this would probably not even be possible for single moms and some other families in our current economic situation, but I believe this is God's ideal.

Another interesting tradition in the ancient Hebrew culture is that children were frequently not weaned until after the first year. In our modern culture this would seem very strange, but I believe God had a purpose in this practice. Because they nursed for so long, babies learned to trust and depend on their mothers. Dependence is a natural phase of healthy emotional and spiritual development. Children who learn to depend on a mom to meet their needs develop a healthy sense of being loved and valued, and later in life they have an ability to trust others to help meet their needs.

On the other hand, children who never learn to depend upon a mother may learn to be independent and self-sufficient from an early age. In our modern culture some parents want their children to become independent as quickly as possible. There are two common reasons for this. One reason is social pressure, so they can keep up with those around them. The second reason is that we are very busy people, and we don't want to be bogged down taking care of little children. If we can get our toddlers to do things on their own, that frees us to continue our busy lives.

I suspect that we treat our children just the opposite of how God intended and how the ancient Hebrews treated children. We want small children to become independent as quickly as possible. Then when they become teenagers—the time when God intended for us as parents to release our children to make their own choices as young men and women—we often try to control their choices and make them more dependent.

If children never develop basic trust and security that their needs will be met, then they may instead develop an independent spirit that refuses to receive wise counsel from their parents during their teenage years. This may motivate parents to attempt to control their teenagers' choices. Weaning children a bit later made it almost impossible for an ancient Hebrew child to not learn dependence and basic trust in early childhood. This made for much more secure teenagers, who were far better spiritually and emotionally prepared to be released into adulthood.

IRRATIONAL FEAR OF ABANDONMENT

The physical presence of a mother who comforts and meets her child's needs is a powerful form of blessing. Sometimes the enemy uses even the unavoidable absence of a mother to impart his message deep into the heart of a small child. Understanding this, it is important that we be alert to the devil's schemes and disarm them as soon as we can. More than once I have seen an irrational fear of abandonment sown deep into the heart of a small child simply through the legitimate unavailability of a mother at a traumatic moment in life.

One of the first times I encountered this was when praying for a woman I'll call Jill. She said she frequently experienced an intense, irrational fear of abandonment and of not being cared for or protected. Jill was married to a wonderful, godly husband. However, her husband frequently traveled for business. Many times when Jill's husband would be preparing to leave on a business trip, she would beg him not to go. Jill would tell him, "I'm so afraid you won't come back. The plane might crash, and you could be killed. Or you might be kidnapped." Trying to comfort her, Jill's husband would cite statistics on the safety of modern aviation. He would remind her of how frequently he traveled and that he always returned.

No matter how her husband tried to comfort her, Jill was still terrified every time he left. At times Jill also was fearful that her husband was having an affair and would leave her for someone else. This was extremely hurtful and frustrating for her husband, as he had never even been interested in another woman, nor had he given his wife reason to doubt his commitment to her. Again, no matter how her husband tried, neither reason nor prayer would allay Jill's fear.

Jill and her husband explained their situation to me during a Blessing Generations Experience. The team and I felt led to simply ask the Lord to show Jill when this fear of abandonment began. After waiting on the Lord for just a few seconds, Jill began to shake with fear and cry uncontrollably. When we asked her what she was experiencing, Jill told us the Holy Spirit had reminded her of a terrifying experience that she endured at five years old.

Jill had been taken to the hospital because she needed surgery to correct a serious heart condition. She remembered having significant apprehension just from the concern her parents expressed about the surgery, but this was not the worst part. Jill's parents were not allowed to stay with her in the hospital overnight, so when evening came, all they could do was reassure her that everything would be fine that night and then go home.

Soon after her parents left, an intense fear hit Jill's heart. Here she was, five years old, with a serious medical condition, not knowing whether she was going to live or die, left in an unfamiliar place. She was terrified all night long and felt abandoned and unloved by her parents. The terror worsened through the night as Jill experienced strange noises, unusual smells, and unfamiliar people constantly poking her with needles and putting things in her mouth, nose, and ears.

The heart of this five-year-old girl was crying out, "Where's my dad? Where's my mom? Don't they care about me? Don't they love me? I'm all alone. All the people I love and in whom I have trusted have abandoned me!" The enemy then took advantage of this circumstance to impart an emotional lie deep into Jill's heart, telling her, "The reason your parents aren't here is that they don't love or care about you. You are not important to them, and they will never come back to help you. You're abandoned, and nobody will ever take care of you."

When Jill's parents returned the next morning, they had no idea the terror she had lived through in the night. They reassured her that they were there now and all would be well, but the damage had been done. The enemy had sown a "virus" of irrational fear of abandonment deep into Jill's heart that persisted on into adulthood.

After the Lord brought this experience back to Jill's memory, we were able to ask her to confess the deep feelings of fear to the Lord. We then asked Him what He had wanted to impart to her that night in the hospital when she was a little girl. That day Jill had an amazing encounter with the living, resurrected Lord Jesus Christ, who began to speak His truth to her. He removed the deep-seated fear and replaced it with total peace and security in His love. Perfect loves casts out fear (1 John 4:18). Jill later reported to us that since that time of ministry, she has never again experienced the fear of her husband being killed or not returning from a business trip. Nor has she been afraid that he would leave her for another woman.

Jill's experience again emphasizes the power of a parent's presence, touch, and comfort to bless the identity of a small child and bring a settled sense of peace and security. Even when it is no fault of the parents, the enemy can use their absence to impart a deep fear into the child's heart. This is not something to be worried about but only to be aware of. Had Jill's parents realized the emotional trauma she experienced as a little girl that night in the hospital, they could have prayed for her immediately after the experience and removed the emotional lie and helped her open her heart to receive truth from the Lord. Such prayer would have spared her the pain of having ongoing fear of abandonment in her adult life.

God's Protective Measures in Ancient Hebrew Culture

Like all the other critical times of blessing in a child's life, God gave us a model for blessing our children at infancy and early childhood within ancient Hebrew culture. I have identified four protective measures God placed within biblical Hebrew culture to ensure children were blessed and not cursed at infancy and early childhood.

1. The mother made the infant her top priority in life, not putting ministry, work outside the home, or anything else ahead of the physical and emotional care of her children.

2. Children were weaned from breast-feeding at a later age, creating in the child a greater

dependence upon the mother and an ability to trust another person to meet their needs.

3. The cultural view of marriage as a covenant and children as a blessing from the Lord created a stable environment in which the care and support of children was a priority in the family.

4. The regular practice of honoring the Sabbath as a family allowed parents to bless their children weekly throughout their growing-up years.

I have already explained how the four attitudes and cultural practices mentioned above contributed to the impartation of blessing to small children. However, in today's Western culture we see the opposite of these occurring. Many mothers are very busy with activities outside the home that make her unavailable to her child in early childhood. In addition, most mothers who breast-feed their infants will wean the baby within the first few months and work to make the child quite independent at an early age.

In many families children are not really considered a blessing from the Lord. Parents may resent the fact that their time and energy must be diverted from making money, pursuing ministry, or some other significant activity to care for a small child. Since we have no regular time of weekly family blessing like the honoring of the Sabbath in ancient Hebrew culture, many children today never hear that their parents are pleased with them and believe they can succeed in life. Instead, with no regular time of blessing, children hear mostly words of correction and disappointment from their parents. In early childhood especially, the primary words children hear from their parents are: "No," "Stop that," "Shame on you," "Bad boy/girl," and "Don't do that!"

Imagine how much easier it would be to impart blessing to

our children in infancy and early childhood if we were to reestablish in our families and communities some of the protective measures mentioned above. Wouldn't it be wonderful if some of these practices from ancient Hebrew culture became "normal" to our children and grandchildren by the time they have their own children? It is possible. You can leave a legacy of blessing for your family. The Blessing Toolbox will show you how.

••• BLESSING TOOLBOX •••

Below are some prayers you can pray over your children during infancy and early childhood. These are meant to serve as a guide. You can personalize them as needed.

REMEDIAL PRAYERS TO BREAK THE CURSE

If your child was adopted and wasn't nurtured in infancy

You may recognize that your child has a greater need for physical touch because he lacked nurture. Be sure to give him lots of appropriate physical attention and affection. You may also wish to pray the following over your child if he is still living in your home.

> *Father, we thank You for* [your child's name]. *He is such a blessing to us. Lord, one of Your names is El Shaddai, the one who is more than enough. El Shaddai, we ask you to fill up* [your child's name]'s *heart with Your love. Touch the heart of the little boy/ girl deep inside who needs to be held, cuddled, and loved. Wrap him in your arms right now and let him experience Your extravagant love and care for him.*

I suggest that you now wait in silence and allow the Lord Himself to love your child. You may also want to hug and hold him as you pray. This is probably not something you'll want to pray only once. You'll likely want to repeat it regularly as your child grows up. After waiting before the Lord, you may want to bless your child with these words:

> [Your child's name], *today we bless your infancy and childhood. We bless you with a supernatural security and a great ability to trust God your Father to meet all your needs. We bless you with an ability to trust other people and to know that you will never walk alone. God will always be with you. Today we declare that your heart shall be at rest in the knowledge that you are never alone. Almighty God will walk with you all the days of your life, and you can trust Him with every aspect of your life. We love you and declare over you that the heart of the small child within is blessed by God and shall be in total peace.*

If your child is an adult, you may want to ask if he would be comfortable with you praying this prayer over him even now. The Lord can deeply touch the heart of an adult with His nurturing love many years after childhood.

If you weren't there for your child in his infancy and you now notice that he has an inability to trust others

1. Repent before the Lord for not being available to nurture your child in infancy and early childhood.

> *Father, I acknowledge today that I was not available to provide the love and nurture my son/daughter needed as a small child. Lord, that was wrong, and I repent of not making* [your child's name] *a priority in my life at that time. I can't pay for any damage done to my child as a result of my actions. But*

Jesus Christ already paid for all my sin, shortcomings, faults, and mistakes. Because of Jesus's blood, Father, I ask You to forgive me for any cursing of identity and lack of blessing that came to my son/ daughter in early childhood as a result of my failure. Lord, I now ask that You would fill my son/daughter with Your love and nurture, and do for my child now what I did not do when [your child's name] *was small. I specifically ask You to give* [your child's name] *a new ability to trust You and others to help meet his needs. I trust You, Lord, to do in my son/ daughter those things that I cannot do. Amen.*

2. You may now wish to pray the same prayer of blessing over your son/daughter as included above.

If you cursed the identity of your child during early childhood

1. Repent and ask God to forgive you.

Father, I acknowledge today that I cursed the identity of my son/daughter when he was a small child. Lord, that was wrong, and I repent of not being Your agent to impart Your message into [your child's name]*'s life at that time. I can't pay for the damage done to my son/daughter as a result of my actions. But Jesus Christ already paid for all my sin, shortcomings, faults, and mistakes. Because of Jesus's blood, Father, I ask You to forgive me for any cursing of identity and lack of blessing that came to my son/daughter in early childhood as a result of my failure. Lord, I now ask that You would fill my son/ daughter with Your love and nurture and do for my child now what I did not do when he/she was small. I specifically ask You to give* [your child's name] *a new ability to trust You and others to be available to him and meet his needs. I trust You, Lord, to do in my son/daughter those things that I cannot do.*

2. You may now want to pray the same prayer over your child as included above.

ACTION STEPS AND PREVENTATIVE PRAYERS TO RELEASE THE BLESSING

As I mentioned previously, you can leave a legacy of blessing for your family. Take the steps below to not only bless your children in infancy and early childhood but also to establish a lifestyle of blessing in your family.

1. *Establish a regular weekly time of blessing in your family.* Follow the pattern outlined at the end of chapter 2 for having a weekly meal and time of blessing.

2. *Touch and hold your infant frequently.* Breast-feeding helps create a secure bond between mother and child. If at all possible, it would be wise for a mother to breast-feed her child. In any case, hold, cuddle, and give love to your child throughout the early childhood years. When both parents hug and show appropriate physical affection, it tends to enliven the spirit of the child. Make abundant use of physical expressions of love and blessing to your child.

3. *Make meeting the needs of your small child a priority in your life.* This tends to help establish basic trust in the child's heart. Doing this will also help you establish a culture of blessing in your family.

4. *Speak a blessing over your child several times a day.* You may want to speak a blessing like the one below over your child several times each day.

[Your child's name], *today I bless your life, spirit, soul, and body. I bless you with a supernatural security and a great ability to trust God your Father to meet all your needs. I bless you with an ability to trust other people and to know that you will never walk alone. God will always be with you. Today I declare that your heart shall be at rest in the knowledge that you are never alone but that Almighty God will walk with you all the days of your life. You can trust Him with every aspect of your life.* [Your child's name], *as you grow, you shall increase in wisdom and stature, and find favor with God and man. I love you and declare that you shall prosper in all your ways all the days of your life.*

Chapter 8

BLESSING YOUR CHILD AT THE TIME OF PUBERTY

WHILE EACH OF the seven critical times of blessing are important, puberty is perhaps one of the most impacting times to bless your child. Puberty is when a child is released into his adult identity. The inner image as a man or woman that is established at this critical time will impact the future course of the child's life.

KEY ROLE PLAYER

While both parents are very important at each critical time of blessing, at puberty the father is the primary role player in blessing the child. In all the preceding years Mom is the key parent God uses to impart security and an ability to trust others in the child. However, at puberty and throughout the teen years Dad steps on center stage as the key person God uses to establish gender identity and release the child into his adult destiny.

Every culture of the world has a tradition or ceremony to release a boy into manhood and a girl into womanhood except our modern Western culture. We have no such rite of passage. In virtually every culture the father through his blessing cuts the emotional umbilical cord that links the child to the mother and releases the child into his or her adult identity and destiny. Mothers were not naturally designed to do this any more than fathers were designed to give birth.

God has given fathers and mothers completely different roles to play in their children's lives. Mothers were designed to do two key things: give birth and nurture. Fathers were designed to accomplish two completely different things: establish a child's gender identity and release him into his adult destiny.

Even at conception it is the father's seed that determines the gender of the child. Genetically a female has two X chromosomes (XX), while a male has an X and a Y (XY). So in conception the only chromosome the mother can contribute to the child is an X while the father can contribute either an X or a Y. If the chromosome contributed in the seed of the father is an X, the child will be a female, but the child will be male if the father contributes a Y chromosome.

I have also noticed God's design in the different way men and women hold a baby. Mothers tend to focus a child inward, holding the child toward her and cuddling him, while fathers tend to focus a child outward. Dads usually put the baby in the palm of their hand facing outward, thus showing the baby the outside world.

I also have observed that many couples divorce right before their firstborn reaches puberty (around age twelve or thirteen). Why is this? I believe this is part of a specific strategy of the enemy to remove the father from his children's lives during the teenage years. The father is the anointed and appointed agent to release a boy to be a man and a girl to be a woman. If he is out of the picture, then the devil will be able to use peers, movies, and circumstances to answer the child's key identity question with his false, destructive message.

If a divorce does occur, children most often live with their mother. Frequently in the early teen years the child suddenly says he wants to go live with his dad, and Mom may be horrified. She may respond by saying, "Why on earth would you want to go live with your father? Don't you know that he is a godless, alcoholic heathen? It would be crazy for you to go live with him."

However, there is something in the heart of that child that knows Dad has something he needs. *That something is the father's blessing.* Very few mothers understand this need in the hearts of their children, but it was designed by God to release him or her into manhood or womanhood. I believe the unavailability of a father to bless his children and release them into their adult identities at the time of puberty is one of the reasons God says He hates divorce (Mal. 2:16). Far too many couples choose to divorce without considering the generational consequence it will have on their children and grandchildren.

There is an intense spiritual battle to keep fathers from spiritually and emotionally connecting with their children. This is why the prophet Malachi says, "Behold, I am going to send you Elijah the prophet before the coming of the great and terrible day of the LORD. *He will restore the hearts of the fathers to their children and the hearts of the children to their fathers,* so that I will not come and smite the land with a curse" (Mal. 4:5–6, emphasis added).

This verse is not talking about the heart of a mother being turned toward her children but the heart of the father. Why would this be? As I considered this, it occurred to me that it is not difficult to turn the heart of a mother to her children. In fact, it is difficult to get the heart of a mother to release her children. What is more challenging, especially in the teen years, is to get the father to emotionally connect with his children. He is often focused on his career, finances, sports, and many things other than his children. This is why the verse says God will turn the hearts of fathers to their children as the spirit of Elijah is released on the earth.

As I mentioned earlier, the Lord Jesus Christ did not begin His ministry until He had received the blessing of His heavenly Father. Again, if the father's blessing was so important that Jesus didn't do one miracle, preach one sermon, or begin His ministry until He had received it, how much more important is it for us today?

WHAT ABOUT SINGLE MOMS?

Some single moms may be asking, "What am I to do? The father of my children is not available to bless them. How can my children be blessed and released into their adult destinies?" While a mother can and should bless her children throughout their lives, she really cannot fulfill this role. It is the father who is called to establish adult identity and release his children into their destiny during the teenage years.

However, when a biological father is unavailable, God will identify other men who might fulfill this role in the lives of the children. There might be a godly grandfather, uncle, pastor, teacher, or coach whom a mother could ask to step into this role for her son or daughter. If you are a single mom, I would encourage you to begin asking the Lord whom He has prepared to help you train your child to have godly character and pray a blessing to release him into his adult identity and destiny.

Some mothers have written off their children's fathers as someone who could bless their children because he is not a believer. I would encourage you not to discount the father even if he does not know God or is irresponsible in many areas of life. God may still use him to impart meaningful blessing to his children.

I have heard testimonies from many mothers who were shocked that their child's father agreed to participate in a ceremony to bless his son or daughter at puberty. Others have said God powerfully used a father despite his flaws to bless his child through his words even though he was not a godly man. So if you are separated or divorced, I encourage you to ask your children's father to consider blessing his children even if he has not been responsible in other ways. He still holds a key that God may use to unlock the future for his children even though he may not fully understand what he is doing.

If the father is unwilling or unavailable to bless his children, the body of Messiah is called to step in. (See James 1:27.) Godly men in the church are called to rise up and be fathers to the fatherless. Several pastors have shared with me the life-changing fruit that resulted when they or other godly men in the church took a young man under their wing. They trained and prepared the boy for adulthood and then conducted a blessing ceremony to release that boy into his manhood. I have also seen godly pastors do the same for a young woman and bless her in a ceremony to release her as a woman. Single moms, don't despair. Ask God whom He would like to use, and when and how He would like to bless your children and release them to be men and women of God.

KEY QUESTION TO BE ANSWERED

The key questions that either God or Satan will answer through parents during puberty are: *Do I have what it takes to be a man/woman? Am I adequate to fulfill my calling as a man/ woman?*

If you recall, puberty can be a time of great insecurity. Your life is changing—physically, emotionally, and intellectually. The key message the devil wants to send at this time is, "You are inadequate. You don't have what it takes to be a man/woman. You're not as well developed as other boys/girls your age. You are just a little kid and will never be a real man/woman."

This is a time when teens may be required to change clothes in front of their peers in a locker room for sports teams and physical education classes in school. Everyone is usually checking each other out and sometimes making comments about one another's physical development. The enemy will always see to it that there is at least one kid there to criticize the others. So this is a time of self-consciousness, self-doubt, and awkwardness.

God intended for a father to be there to answer his child's heart question with a resounding, "Yes, you are adequate. You have everything you need to be the man/woman God has called you to be. You are not a little child any more. You are a young man/woman. Nothing more is required. You have what it takes, and this day I release you to be a man/woman!"

Now, men and women tend to perceive value and adequacy in very different ways and thus have slightly different inner heart questions they need their fathers to answer. When a man's heart asks, "Am I adequate?", he usually wants to know, "Am I powerful? Am I a force to be reckoned with? Do I have a purpose to fulfill? Do I have the intelligence and skills to fulfill that purpose—to do something significant—and will my work really make a difference on the earth? Would someone actually pay me significant money for my ideas and/or skills? Do I have what it takes to attract a woman who will unite with me in my life's purpose and calling? Do I really have what it takes to fulfill a wife sexually, emotionally, and financially, to protect her and provide for her, or will I be found lacking?"

When a woman's heart asks, "Am I adequate?", she usually wants to know, "Am I beautiful and enchanting? Am I worth pursuing? Am I attractive enough (spiritually, emotionally, and sexually) for a man to risk his life to pursue and fight for me? Is there a man who will love me so much that he would kill the dragon, swim the moat, scale the castle wall, kill the evil prince, rescue me from the tower, and take me off on a white horse into the adventure of a lifetime? Or will I be alone all my life because I am too fat, ugly, or stupid for anyone to ever want me?"

A father is the one who can impart God's answer to these key questions into the heart of his son or daughter at puberty. How that father relates to his daughter at this critical time in life establishes an expectation in her heart of how she will be treated by men in general and by her future husband specifically. How the father relates to his son establishes in his heart an expectation of how he will be treated by employers and others in the marketplace.

BLESSING AND CURSING AT PUBERTY

Every culture in the world has ceremonies, traditions, and rites of passage at puberty to release a boy to be a man and a girl to be a woman. While the traditions and ceremonies may vary from culture to culture, the basic elements of blessing remain the same.

Blessing at the time of puberty may include:

1. The parents learning to separate identity from behavior in order to bless the identity of the son/ daughter even while correcting his behavior

2. The parents creating a safe home environment, which facilitates the open sharing of feelings and experiences between the father and the son or daughter

3. The father accepting and blessing his child in a correct and healthy way, thereby severing the childhood identity from the mother and releasing his son/daughter into manhood/womanhood

4. An initiation into manhood/womanhood that the father orchestrates

Cursing at the time of puberty may include:

1. The parents shaming and cursing the child's identity while attempting to correct his behavior

2. The father preventing the children from openly sharing their feelings and experiences with him because of divorce or his ignorance, insecurity, apathy, desertion, death, or the like

3. The father not accepting, blessing, or releasing his children, and the identity of the son or daughter remaining bound to the mother, causing the son/daughter to still feel like a child even into adulthood

4. The father manifesting an attitude of shame or embarrassment over the physical changes in his son or daughter

5. The son or daughter experiencing physical, emotional, or sexual abuse, resulting in a feeling of uncleanness and worthlessness

Potential Consequences
of Blessing and Cursing at Puberty

It is God's intent that every son and daughter receive a powerful impartation of identity and destiny from his or her father at the time of puberty. I believe this impartation is to come in the form of a public, ceremonial blessing. This blessing empowers the son or daughter to prosper in adulthood and brings emotional closure to childhood. The father and/or other key men in the community of believers are the ones who are appointed and anointed to impart this blessing.

In Hebrew tradition the son or daughter who is released into adulthood is called a bar mitzvah (son) or bat mitzvah (daughter), meaning "son or daughter of the commandment." As I was seeking the Lord for a term we might use in our new covenant culture, I came upon the Hebrew phrase *bar barakah* (or *bat barakah*), which means "son (or daughter) of the blessing." This phrase has become popular in many congregations that have made blessing at the time of puberty a regular part of their congregational culture. But it is not so important what you call the experience so long as you make it a regular part of your family and community culture.

I have found three key components to the blessing at the time of puberty: instruction, ceremony, and celebration. We will look at each in more detail later in the Blessing Toolbox, but right now I want to discuss the concept of ceremony because I believe this is a crucial element of the blessing.

CEREMONY BRINGS
SPIRITUAL AND EMOTIONAL CLOSURE

I believe we have lost the value of ceremony in our modern Western culture. A ceremony tends to bring spiritual and emotional closure to a phase of life, and it often releases an individual into a new phase. This is true of a wedding ceremony. A legitimate wedding ceremony brings spiritual, emotional, and physical closure to single life and releases the couple into married life. I believe God intended for the ceremonial blessing at the time of puberty to bring the same type of emotional closure to childhood and release that individual into life as an adult.

In cultures that regularly have rites of passage ceremonies, the young man or woman does experience spiritual and emotional closure and release into a new phase of life. For example, in Orthodox Jewish culture, if you ask a teenager, "Are you a man?", he will answer definitively yes or no. Why? Because there will be a ceremony (bar mitzvah) that releases him to be a man. After that day he will dress differently and have privileges and responsibilities he did not have before. In most cases the boy's feelings actually change at that time as well.

On the other hand, I have discovered that many people who have never been ceremonially blessed at the time of puberty retain feelings of being a little boy or girl into adulthood. If you ask people, "When does one become a man/woman?", their answers likely will vary. I've heard people say, "At age eighteen," "At age twenty-one," "When you learn to drive," "When you get married," "When you first have sex," "When you have a child," and more. The point is that no one really knows.

In reality, God intended for the ceremonial blessing of the father to spiritually and emotionally release a boy to be a man or a girl to be a woman. Without that blessing many people spend a lifetime waiting to finally feel like an adult. That feeling will not go away at any particular age because God designed it to end when the child's emotional umbilical cord is cut through a ceremonial blessing that the father leads. You may recall the story about Luis, who felt and behaved like an angry little boy until his sixty-fifth birthday when his father blessed him and released him to be a man. On that day Luis actually felt like a man for the first time in his life. God had intended for this to happen some fifty years earlier, but unfortunately, though they were Christians, this family did not grow up in a culture of blessing.

In some cultures fathers understand that they are responsible to release their sons to be men but do so in perverted ways. Some men have told me that in their mid-teen years, their dads took them out to get drunk and arranged to have them spend a night with a prostitute to initiate their sex life. Rather than generating a confident feeling of manhood, the actions of these fathers only led to feelings of guilt, shame, defilement, and addiction.

People whose fathers never released them into adulthood at puberty try to *do* something they think will make the feeling of being a child go away. Men may join a gang, which has its own rite of passage through which boys become men. They may join the military or attempt to achieve success in sports or their careers. A woman may do similar things seeking to become a "real woman." She may become promiscuous trying to attract men, or also seek financial status or athletic or career success. None of these will ever substitute for a father's blessing or dispel the insecure feelings of childhood.

GOD'S PROTECTIVE MEASURES IN ANCIENT HEBREW CULTURE

God placed two key protective measures in ancient Hebrew to ensure children were blessed at puberty:

1. A rite of passage ceremony practiced at puberty

2. The Law of Moses (Torah), which taught parents by practical example to separate identity from behavior and how to govern by offering choices with consequences rather than by cursing identity in an attempt to control behavior

In ancient Hebrew culture every family held a ceremony to release a child into his adult identity. Every son and most daughters were expected to pass through a rite of passage ceremony on their twelfth or thirteenth birthday. At that time the father would bless the child, and the community would receive him into the fellowship of adults. While there was almost always a ceremony to release a boy to be a man, unfortunately there was not always such a ceremony for the girls. As we incorporate this blessing tradition into our families and communities, we must realize that girls need this blessing just as much as boys do.

God used the blessing of the father at puberty to seal inside the young man or woman an appropriate adult gender identity. Even today in Hebrew culture and other cultures that practice rite of passage ceremonies, there seems to be very little gender confusion. In contrast, because of the blessing deficit in our modern culture, we see a great deal of gender confusion in adult life.

A second protective measure God placed in ancient Hebrew culture was the cultural acceptance of the Law of Moses (the Torah). In the first five books of the Bible God taught His people His system of governing, which was to offer choices with consequences (Deut. 30:19). By giving a commandment, teaching, and prescribing a consequence for violation (Prov. 6:23), God taught parents and families by example how to separate identity from behavior. Thus there was a great chance if you grew up in this culture that your parents would have used God's system of government rather than Satan's to govern your behavior in the family.

Today many parents repeat the pattern of past generations and use Satan's system of control to govern the behavior of their children in the teenage years. Again, we can change this in our families for the next generation.

••• BLESSING TOOLBOX •••

As in the previous chapters I want to share some specific prayers you can pray over your children at the time of puberty. We will begin with remedial prayers you can pray if you failed to bless your children at puberty and they are now past that age. We will then look in some detail at how you can bless your son or daughter at the time of puberty.

REMEDIAL PRAYERS TO BREAK THE CURSE

If you missed the opportunity to bless your child at puberty and he or she is much older now, plan to conduct a ceremony to release your child into adulthood.

It is important to realize that your child's heart still longs to receive the blessing of a father that cuts the spiritual and emotional umbilical cord that ties him to his mother and releases him into his adult identity.

It doesn't matter how old your son or daughter is. Remember Luis, whose life was changed when he received his father's blessing at age sixty-five? If you are still breathing and your adult child is still breathing, then I encourage you to conduct a blessing ceremony and celebration. If your child is already an adult, you may not want to include some of the components I outline in the next section, such as the time of instruction. It's OK to adapt this to fit your family. What is most important is that you conduct the blessing ceremony and celebration.

If you cursed rather than blessed your child at puberty, repent of being Satan's agent to impart his message in the life of your child.

Then plan to conduct a blessing ceremony and celebration to release your son/daughter into adulthood. You can use the prayer below as a guide for asking God's forgiveness for cursing your offspring.

> *Father, we recognize today that during the time of* [your child's name]'s *adolescence we were used by the enemy to curse his identity and take his value. That was not Your message. Today we renounce the message imparted at that time through our words, attitudes, and actions. Father, forgive us by the blood of Jesus for not imparting Your message to our son/daughter. Forgive us for not conducting a proper ceremony to release our son/daughter into his manhood/womanhood. We now break the power of any curse we released over* [your child's name]'s *manhood/womanhood. Lord, we ask You now to speak to* [your child's name]'s *spirit the truth of who he/she is as a man/woman. We declare that* [your child's

name] *is no longer a little child—is not his mother's little boy/girl—but is a man/woman.*

PRAYERS AND ACTION STEPS TO RELEASE THE BLESSING

The rest of the Blessing Toolbox will explain how to bless your son or daughter at the time of puberty. I mentioned earlier that three key components should be included in the act of blessing a son or daughter at puberty and releasing him or her into adult identity. For a more detailed description of each component, see my book *Bar Barakah: A Parent's Guide to a Christian Bar Mitzvah.*[1]

INSTRUCTION

The blessing ceremony at the time of puberty for either a boy or a girl should include a time of preparation and instruction by the parents. This time of instruction is as important as the ceremony itself. Unfortunately, because many of us did not receive this type of instruction from our parents, it is sometimes hard to know what to say to our children at this time. Thus it may be helpful to first consult your pastor as you would if your child were getting married.

However, as I mentioned before, it is your responsibility to instruct your children, not the pastor's. Let him provide some guidelines for you, but don't turn the instruction over to him. The pastor or youth pastor will not stand before God to give an account for the instruction given to your children. You will.

I believe the father is to initiate and oversee this instruction, but both parents should participate if that is possible. God created a beautiful window of opportunity for this instruction, and that is in the year or two preceding the onset of adolescence. At around age eleven or twelve most children are uniquely prepared by God to receive instruction about adulthood from their parents. Children's hearts still tend to be very open to their parents at that time in life, as they are not yet consumed with as many extracurricular activities. Most children also still enjoy spending time with their parents at that age.

Although information and teaching are important, these times of instruction should be more focused on building relationship and mentoring than on imparting content. This instruction time is meant to prepare the child:

1. To enter into a settled sense of adult identity

2. To develop a clear sense of destiny and purpose, including an initial personal mission statement

3. To be emotionally released into manhood or womanhood during the blessing ceremony

4. To take adult responsibility for his own spiritual health from the time of the ceremony on

5. To walk in emotional and sexual purity all the days of his life

Let us talk now about how parents might conduct the actual instruction time with their son or daughter. One of the critical responsibilities of parents is to give their children age-appropriate information about sex. While there are many other important topics to discuss with your children when they are approaching puberty, discussions about sex and the changes in their bodies are particularly important—and typically the most awkward. It will help to remember that discussions about sex should happen throughout a child's growing-up years, not just at one time.

I believe it is God's intention for a father to be the primary source of sexual information for both his son and daughter. They are not meant to learn sexual misinformation from peers, other adults, video games, websites, or movies. While it is important that both parents participate in the sexual education of their children, it is especially important when preparing to release his children into their adult identity that the father has several open discussions on this topic.

When it comes to talking with their daughters about sex, many fathers, out of their own insecurity and embarrassment, delegate this task to the mother. This is not healthy. As I have mentioned, the way a father relates to his daughter at this critical time in life prepares her spiritually and emotionally for a relationship with her husband. If her father shuns her sexuality and femininity as shameful or embarrassing, the daughter will tend to expect the same from her future husband. This is why it is very important for a father to be involved in talking with his daughter about her growing sexuality.

When talking with a son about sex as he approaches puberty, the father could tell his son something like this: "Son, in the next few months to a year you will notice physical, emotional, and intellectual changes in your life. You will find yourself thinking thoughts that you have never had before. You will find yourself feeling some emotions that you have never felt before. You will begin to grow hair on parts of your body where you have never had hair before.

"Son, in the next little while, you will begin to care deeply how you look to other people, especially girls. I know this may not make any sense to you right now, but I want you to remember what I am telling you for the future. You will find yourself wanting to spend time with girls, and you will experience feelings of sexual attraction toward them. Son, I want you to know that these changes are of God, not the devil. God is the one who made us sexual beings, and sexual attraction in and of itself is not dirty or unclean. It is good, right, and pure.

"God created you to be sexually attracted to women. However, son, there is a difference between sexual attraction and lust. If you do not learn how to handle sexual thoughts properly, they will develop into lust, which is not of God and will destroy your life. I know what I am talking about, son, because I have had to deal with these same thoughts and feelings myself. I want to teach you how to talk to Jesus Christ and release these thoughts and feelings to Him. Son, when you begin to have such thoughts and feelings, I want you to start talking to me about these things, because I can help you to handle them properly. OK? I want to walk with you through this time in your life."

A father should be able to speak to his daughter in a similar way: "Honey, you are growing up, and in the next few months to a year you will experience many things changing in your life. You will begin to have thoughts you never had before and experience some emotions you have never felt before. You will begin to have feelings of sexual attraction toward boys. This is not wrong or evil. It is natural and designed by God. Sexual relationship is not something dirty, unclean, or impure. However, if you do not learn how to release your sexual thoughts and emotions to Jesus, Satan will try to develop this God-given attraction into lust. Lust is impure and is very destructive.

"As you grow, because God made you very beautiful, you will find many young men who approach you in a sexual way because they are motivated by lust. You may feel like you have to protect yourself continually from them. However, God never intended for you to have to protect your own heart from the lust of young men. God placed me in your life to be the protector of your emotional and sexual purity. Therefore, if you find a young man flirting with you or expressing interest in having more than a friendship with you, please just give him my business card and tell him to make an appointment with me. I will be happy to meet with him to determine if he is sent from God as a potential marriage partner for you.

"Honey, in the next few months to a year you will also

experience many changes in your physical body. You will begin to grow hair in places where you have previously had none. You will also one day find yourself vaginally bleeding. I know that this is somewhat embarrassing to talk about, but I want you to know that this is completely normal. When it happens, I do not want you to be scared or to think that you are dying or are really sick. This is normal and was designed by God to happen to every girl as she becomes a woman. This bleeding is part of a normal cycle of life that cleanses your body and will give you the ability to bear children one day. You do not have to be afraid of it or embarrassed about it. When this cycle begins in your body, your mom and I want to celebrate with you, because this will begin to mark your transition from being a little girl into being a woman."

If you will have this type of open discussion with your son and daughter, you will move toward keeping an open relationship with them over the next few years. This will enable you to continue to bless and guide them as they learn to walk in their own adult identity and destiny. It may seem like I am describing "the talk" about sex, but that is not my intent. My hope is that over the years you will seize many opportunities to have these kinds of discussions with your children.

CEREMONY

The time of instruction, which may last several months to a year, is meant to culminate in a blessing ceremony that releases the son or daughter into adulthood. This ceremony helps to create an emotional closure to childhood. As I mentioned earlier, this ceremony is no small thing and should be treated like a very important event. In Jewish culture this ceremony is frequently made as high a priority as a wedding. In his book *Raising a Modern-Day Knight*, Robert Lewis outlines four key components of a significant blessing ceremony.[2]

1. *It is costly.* Something that costs you nothing conveys little value. King David wanted to erect an altar to the Lord on the threshing floor of Araunah the Jebusite. Araunah offered to give his threshing floor to the king, but David told Araunah, "'No, but I will surely buy it from you for a price, for I will not offer burnt offerings to the LORD my God which cost me nothing.' So David bought the threshing floor and the oxen for fifty shekels of silver" (2 Sam. 24:24). David understood that the expenditure of money conveys value. I am not suggesting that you must spend tens of thousands of dollars on the blessing ceremony, but I do believe that the expenditure should be significant.

2. *It ascribes value to the individual.* By "making a big deal" out of the blessing ceremony, you are telling your child, "You are important. This moment is important."

3. *It should employ meaningful symbols.* There should be a tangible token that your child will keep to mark the bar barakah. This may be a ring or locket, an article of clothing, a certificate, or some other physical token. Some primitive people groups would make permanent marks on their bodies when they passed through a meaningful ceremony. I personally believe that much of the body piercing among young people today is due to a lack of a father's blessing to release them into their adult identity. For many young people body piercings and tattoos are simply an expression of the legitimate need for a unique, visible

token of manhood/womanhood that was never properly given by a father.

4. *It empowers the life with vision.* A memorable ceremony creates a moment of transition. It conveys in a powerful way the message, "Your life will never be the same. You are entering a new season." This happened for Jesus when He was baptized in the Jordan River. It happens for a Jewish son at his bar mitzvah ceremony, and it happens for every married couple at the wedding ceremony. We want to convey to our children at their blessing ceremony, "Your life will be totally different from now on. You will never be a little boy/girl again."

A tradition that has become popular in some congregations is a weekend father-son retreat in the woods. This is to release and welcome the sons into the community of men. Some communities also like including a "princess ball" as a part of the ceremony to release their daughters into womanhood. I believe these kinds of events are quite valuable, as it is important to pursue the journey into manhood or womanhood in community with others. It also is important to spread the culture of blessing beyond your own family and into the community of believers.

It is beyond the scope of this book to go into more detail about the ceremony itself. If you would like more specific instruction on how to plan a blessing ceremony, you may want to read my book *Bar Barakah: A Parent's Guide to a Christian Bar Mitzvah.*

I believe the ceremony should include commitments from the child as well as blessings from the parents, particularly the father. Below I will include several sample commitments and blessings that I believe are wise to include in the ceremony.

These samples were modified from the actual ones my wife and I used with our two sons, Josh and Johnny, in their blessing ceremonies. These commitments can be adapted for use with either a son or daughter.

Sample commitments to be made by the child

1. I commit the rest of my life to the Lord Jesus Christ. My desire is for Him to make me the man/woman He wants me to be.

2. I commit to live my life, as God gives me His grace, in a manner that is pleasing to Him, embracing the Bible as my absolute standard for faith and conduct and the basis for all decisions I make in my life.

3. I commit as a single young man/woman to relate to women/men in a pure and godly way. I choose to conduct my relationships with women/men in accordance with the principles of godly friendships and partnership as opposed to dating. (I will discuss this concept at length in chapter 9.)

4. As I am released today as a man/woman, I commit to continue to honor the authority of my parents and to view them as God's primary instruments of character growth and development in my life.

5. I commit to recognize money as a gift from God rather than something I have earned. As such, I commit to the godly stewardship of all financial resources God may choose to make available to me. I specifically renounce the spirit of mammon and choose to make Jesus Christ the source of my financial provision from this day forward.

6. I choose to honor all legitimate authority in my life. I commit to honor the authority of my parents, teachers, pastors, and civil authorities. I specifically renounce the attitude or lifestyle of independence and rebellion, and I choose to live my life as a free man/woman, abiding under authority and exercising authority.

7. My favorite scripture up to this point in my life is _____.

Sample commitments to be made by parents

1. We commit to continue to teach you God's principles of life.

2. We commit to continue to love you. There is nothing you can ever do that will cause us not to love you. You will always be our son/daughter.

3. We commit to make it a priority to be available to you for counsel in any area of your life at any time. We will listen to you without judgment or condemnation and do everything within our power to cooperate with God in blessing your life.

4. We commit to pray for you regularly. We will continue to pray for God's will to be accomplished in your life and for you to fulfill your destiny in Him.

5. We commit to partner with you in prayer regarding God's choice and timing in a wife/husband for you. We agree to protect you from any woman/man not sent by God to be your wife/husband.

6. We commit to continue to honor you with open communication and understanding. As God gives us grace, we will attempt to always

separate identity from behavior so as to honor you as a person even when your behavior requires discipline.

7. We commit to continue to apply age-appropriate, godly discipline to your life, as the Lord directs, for character development and training to fulfill your destiny as long as you remain in our home.

Sample prayer of a father's blessing

Many people have asked me for a sample of the father's blessing to be prayed over a child in a blessing ceremony. Obviously there is no standard prayer, as each parent must pray as the Holy Spirit leads. However, in order to give you some direction, I have enclosed the following guidelines and sample prayer of blessing.

A sample blessing to pray over a young person at the bar/bat barakah ceremony should include at least the following five components:

1. A confirmation of gender identity

2. A release into manhood or womanhood

3. A calling forth of positive character qualities

4. A proclamation of any prophetic words that have been given over the son or daughter

5. A pronouncement of specific personal blessing of the father and mother to the child

The blessing a father would pray over his son, Bob, might sound something like this:

Father God, I thank You for my son, Bob. Bob, you are no longer a little boy. Today you have become a man. You are well equipped with everything you

need to fulfill your destiny as a man of God. Before the foundation of the earth God Almighty planned for you to be a man. There is nothing that you will ever need to do to become a man because God has made you one. Today we are simply recognizing publicly what God has done in you.

Also note specific character qualities in the child, for example:

Bob, I have noticed that God has made you very intelligent. He has also given you a gift of articulate speech and an ability to take complicated concepts and make them simple for others to understand. I believe the Lord will use you powerfully to teach His Word to others. You also are a peacemaker. I notice that when your friends are at odds with one another, God frequently gives you just the right words to help them reconcile. I believe God will use you greatly in these areas of reconciliation and teaching.

Son, I am so glad that God has given you to our family. You are a wonderful son. I love you! Today I am so proud of you. I bless you with wisdom from God, with emotional security, with sexual purity, and marital fidelity. May God continue to prosper you in all that you do, and may you serve the Lord Jesus Christ all the days of your life. Today I loose you from being your mother's little boy, and I release to you the authority and responsibility of manhood. Bob, today before God and these witnesses, as your father I declare that you are a man. I love you, son, and I release you to fulfill your destiny in Christ.

CELEBRATION

No ceremony is complete without a party afterward to celebrate. This bar/bat barakah celebration could be much like a wedding reception. Again, I will make some suggestions, but you need to design a reception for your child appropriate to your own culture. Most people do not need much instruction on how to have a party.

I believe this reception should be at the same type of venue you would hold a wedding reception. You may wish to serve dinner or just light refreshments. In any case, you may want to have a cake to honor your son/daughter. It is entirely appropriate for the guests to bless the young man or woman with gifts or money (perhaps toward future education or missions trips). You may also want to have a praise and worship band present to provide music.

After the guests have eaten and fellowshipped for a while, you may want to open the floor to allow the guests to further bless your child. Perhaps you will want to speak some more informal words of blessing, or you may want to ask specific individuals to share a scripture, prophetic word, prayer, poem, song, or story about your child. It is important that anything shared serve to bless and edify your child. Stories or words that embarrass, belittle, or shame would not be appropriate.

Remember that everything I have shared in this Blessing Toolbox is just a boilerplate from which you may develop your own blessing tradition in your family and community. It is far less important how you do it than that you do it. So I encourage you not to spend too much time trying to get it "just right." Ask God how He wants you to bless your children, and He will direct you.

Chapter 9

BLESSING YOUR CHILD AT THE TIME OF MARRIAGE

W̳E NOW COME to the sixth critical time of blessing in the life of a son or daughter. This is the blessing God intended to occur at the time of marriage. Not every son or daughter is called by God to be married, but most are. Just as a significant transition occurs at puberty from childhood to adulthood, another important transition takes place at the time of marriage from single life to married life. I believe God intended for every marriage to be blessed by both sets of parents. However, for many reasons in our culture today many couples are not blessed in marriage by their parents.

KEY ROLE PLAYER

Both parents play a key role in blessing their children's marriage and releasing their son or daughter to be joined to a spouse. Either parent has the ability to bless and release or to curse and retain. This is why we have found it very important to include parents in the marriage preparation process. If parents understand their scriptural role to bless and release, it will make the transition from single life to married life much easier for the newly married couple.

KEY QUESTION TO BE ANSWERED

The key questions to be answered by God or Satan at the time of marriage are: *Am I really loveable? Do I really have what it takes to be someone's wife/husband? Will anyone love me and stick with me in covenant long-term?* Since marriage is a lifelong covenant, many people experience great fear about choosing the right person.

Parents have an opportunity at this time to tell their son or daughter, "Yes, you are completely adequate and prepared to be a husband/wife. You have everything you need spiritually, emotionally, and physically. We have prayed since the day you were born for God to bring you His choice of a wife/husband, and now He has. This is the right person at the right time, and we bless your marriage and future life together."

Unfortunately many parents are unable to bless the marriage of their son or daughter with integrity because they don't truly believe the bride- or groom-to-be is God's choice or that their child is ready to marry. Thus many parents are faced with the dilemma of either blessing a marriage they don't really believe in or withholding their blessing.

It was so important to God that parents bless their children's marriage that He put a protective provision in ancient Hebrew culture that made it almost impossible for a marriage not to be blessed by parents. In biblical Hebrew culture the parents were deeply involved in selecting their children's marriage partner. In some cases the parents chose their son's or daughter's spouse without giving their child much choice. Since the parents chose the marriage partners, they virtually always approved of the marriage.

I am not suggesting that we return to arranged marriages. I am merely making the point that it was so important to God that parents bless the marriage of their children that He made it almost impossible for that not to happen in biblical Hebrew culture. Even in our culture today I believe God wants families to learn to partner together in managing romantic relationships and selecting a marriage partner. If parents and their son or daughter are praying and seeking God together for God to bring His choice of a marriage partner, there is a much better chance the parents will bless the marriage than if the parents are not involved in the process. When sons and daughters manage their own romantic relationships and potential marriage partner selection process in isolation from their parents, there is a much greater chance that son or daughter will miss God's plan for a marriage partner.

Blessing and Cursing
at the Time of Marriage

Almost every culture in the world embraces the concept of marriage in some form. In most cultures the blessing of the parents at a wedding plays a key role in releasing the newly married couple to prosper in their new life together.

Blessing at the time of marriage may include the following key components:

1. Both sets of parents being in agreement with their son or daughter about the choice of marriage partner and the timing of the marriage

2. Both sets of parents attending the wedding ceremony and blessing the marriage

3. Each set of parents joyfully receiving the new son-/daughter-in-law as a part of their family

4. Both sets of parents willingly releasing their son/daughter spiritually and emotionally to be joined to a wife/husband to become a new family unit

Cursing at the time of marriage may entail such things as:

1. Either or both sets of parents disagreeing with their child's choice of a marriage partner or with the timing of the marriage, and maintaining that

the person is the wrong choice and the marriage won't last

2. Either or both sets of parents refusing to attend the wedding ceremony and refusing to bless or actively cursing the marriage of their son/daughter

3. Either or both sets of parents rejecting the new son-/daughter-in-law and refusing to receive him/her into their family

4. Either or both sets of parents refusing to allow their son/daughter to emotionally or spiritually leave father and mother, thus blocking their child from appropriately being joined to the wife/husband as a new family unit

POTENTIAL CONSEQUENCES OF BLESSING AND CURSING IN MARRIAGE

Let's now look at some of the consequences of blessing and cursing in marriage. When both sets of parents bless a marriage, it usually brings the children a greater sense of peace and security. They have nothing to prove to their parents and are able to let the Holy Spirit lead them in their marriage.

On the other hand, when parents have cursed their children's marriage, the children are highly motivated to disprove the problems the parents foresaw. If the parents have said such things as, "This marriage won't last six months," "You're marrying the wrong person," or "You're too young to get married," then children will commonly want to prove them wrong.

When parents make statements such as these—words that curse the identity of a son or daughter—the child's soul will certainly be out of peace. Because the adult child is working to disprove the parents' words, his heart is not free to be led by the Holy Spirit in marriage. Instead the flesh is continually motivating the child to bring peace to his soul by proving the parents wrong. Both individuals in the marriage then labor under the curse of the parents to attempt to disprove their words.

A second consequence is that children who were not blessed by their parents in marriage usually don't develop a friendship with their parents and therefore can't enjoy a close relationship with them throughout their adult lives. This may strain the relationship with any grandchildren who may be born.

Blessing Looses While Cursing Binds

Yet another consequence of parents not blessing an adult child's marriage is that the married son or daughter cannot properly leave the parents and be joined to a wife or husband. Blessing tends to give the child the spiritual and emotional ability to leave father and mother, while cursing tends to bind the heart of a child spiritually and emotionally to the parents. In ministering to thousands of married couples through the years, I have discovered that much marital conflict is rooted in an inability to properly cleave (be joined) to a spouse because the individual's heart never spiritually and emotionally left his parents. (See Genesis 2:24.) When one doesn't leave, it is impossible to cleave. Obviously this is not a geographic leaving but a spiritual and emotional one.

God designed men to be secure in their masculine identity through their parents' blessing and then to lead, protect, and fight for their wives. Yet a man who has not been blessed by his parents will usually look to his wife to make him feel like a man. Such a man will not lead, protect, and fight for his wife. Instead he will protect himself, fight with his wife, and abdicate his leadership in the family.

God designed a woman to trust her husband to protect and fight for her, thus allowing her to respect and submit to him. A woman who has never been blessed by her parents will usually not trust her husband because she could not trust her father. Because of this distrust, she will neither respect nor submit to her husband. Instead she will protect herself, fight with her husband, and undermine or usurp his authority in the family.

As I have ministered to married couples, I have found that many times a primary mechanism that binds the heart of an adult child to a parent is the child's judgment and bitterness. Hebrews 12:15 tells us that bitterness in my heart will defile not only me but many other people as well. How does this work?

Unfortunately the human soul is like a camera and reproduces deep inside the image of its focus. You cannot focus your camera on the lion at the zoo but desire and expect the camera to produce a photo of the elephant. You will get a picture of the lion upon which you focused the camera, not the elephant you desired. Desire does not produce image; emotional focus does. Judgment and bitterness create deep inside an emotional focus on the very quality judged in another, regardless of the intention to produce in one's own life just the opposite. Thus while growing up, if a child is treated with injustice and cursing and is never blessed by parents, he may judge and isolate from his parents in his heart.

This child then goes into marriage with an image deep in the heart containing negative qualities judged in a parent. Because of the principle of sowing and reaping (every seed reproduces after its own kind), this image has potential to reproduce in the life of the adult child the very qualities hated in the parent. Or worse yet, an adult child may tend to view his marriage partner through the negative image of the judged parent, thus creating an unconscious expectation that the spouse will become just like the parent. This seed of bitterness in the heart then may reproduce in the marriage partner the exact qualities judged in a parent. Let me give you a practical example.

Seed Always Bears Fruit After Its Own Kind

Suppose a young woman named Mary grows up with a hyper-critical father, whom she judges. She then vows to never marry a critical man like her father. Meanwhile a young man named Tom grows up with an undisciplined, obese mother, whom he judges. He then vows to never marry an overweight woman like his mother.

These two young people meet and marry. Tom is very accepting and kind—nothing like Mary's father. Mary has a beautiful figure, unlike Tom's mother, and is also a wonderful cook. In an attempt to bless her husband, Mary cooks wonderful meals every evening. However, the food she cooks is a little too rich for her, and she gains a couple of pounds. Because Tom is yet bound in his heart to his mother, without realizing it he views Mary through the image of his mother. Her small weight gain greatly alarms him, and he gently confronts his wife about her figure. Mary, who is still bound in her heart to her dad, hears Tom's words through the image of her father. Being deeply wounded by Tom's criticism, Mary reacts with a very emotional response. A serious argument then ensues as Tom continues to express his deep concern about Mary's weight.

Being under the additional emotional pressure of her husband's criticism, Mary begins snacking a little between meals and gains another couple of pounds. Tom, of course, is now even more alarmed and confronts Mary again, resulting in another highly emotional argument. If Tom and Mary never identify and repent of the way their hearts are still bound to their parents through judgment and bitterness, their marriage will soon consist of a very disappointed and critical husband and a very wounded and overweight wife.

My family once lived next to a woman who was about to divorce her third husband. When I asked her what her experience had been with her three husbands, she proceeded to tell me that they all had manifested the same types of addictions and serious dysfunction that her father had dealt with. I asked her if these three men were like that before she married them. She acknowledged that the first one had some of those characteristics, but that neither of the others had behaved that way at all before they married her.

I asked this woman to what she attributed marrying three different men who all demonstrated the same negative character qualities she had despised in her father. My neighbor replied by saying, "I guess I just don't know how to pick them." As I heard her story, I wanted to ask, "Did you ever think you might be the one carrying the seed? It doesn't much matter what field you plant it in. Until you recognize and deal with it in your life, that seed of judgment and bitterness toward your father will yield the same fruit every time." I realized that she, unfortunately, was not yet ready to hear that word.

You're Just Like My Mother!

Let me give you one more example of a couple for whom I prayed several years ago. A man I'll call Jim decided to cut himself off from his mother and managed to reproduce in his wife the very qualities he hated in his mom. Jim's wife came to me for help first, saying she loved Jim deeply but was considering divorce because circumstances in the marriage had made her life intolerable. She said Jim refused to take any type of responsibility at home. Now the bank was about to repossess their house, not because they didn't have enough money to pay the mortgage but because Jim "never got around" to making the payment.

Jim knew it was his job to pay the bills, keep the yard, maintain the cars, shovel the walks in the winter, and so on, but he never really did any of those things. Consequently Jim's wife had begrudgingly taken over all of those responsibilities and was extremely weary and frustrated.

I met Jim the following week. Initially I asked him how his marriage was going. He replied, "Oh, we have our ups and downs like everyone else, but we really love each other and have a good, stable marriage. I can't really complain about anything." There was quite a disparity between his and his wife's perception of the marriage. Jim was shocked when I told him that his wife was considering divorce.

I confronted Jim about the irresponsibility his wife reported. He acknowledged that he just seemed to "space out" all the time. At first I began to work with Jim on time management and goal setting, but try as I might, he still never fulfilled his responsibilities around the house. I began to understand his wife's frustration.

I then realized that there was a much deeper root. After we prayed together to ask the Lord to reveal the root of this problem, I felt led to ask Jim several questions about his mother, and the answers began to come. Jim was the younger of two children. His mother clearly favored his older sister and conveyed a message to him that he couldn't do anything right.

Jim's mother wanted to spare him the embarrassment of making any mistakes, so she constantly redid everything he attempted so that it would be "right." When she asked Jim to set the table for dinner, she always came behind him and reset it after him because it was never to her satisfaction. She also instilled in him the belief that making a mistake was a terrible thing that should be avoided at all costs.

Every time Jim's mom would redo one of his tasks and criticize him for the job he had done, it deeply wounded his heart. It was a form of cursing his identity and was very painful emotionally. It taught Jim from a very early age that he couldn't do anything to please his mother, so the best way to avoid being hurt and criticized was to not do anything at all for her. After that point he was scolded for not completing the task he had been given, but to Jim that was far less painful than being chastised for doing it "wrong." Besides, his mom would come and do it the way she wanted anyway, so the task would still be accomplished.

When Jim married, what kind of woman do you think he looked for? You are right—someone who was the exact opposite of his mother. He found a wonderful Christian girl who loved Jim just the way he was and never criticized him as his mom used to do. Of course, Jim's wife did not meet his mother's expectations, and she constantly told him he could have done much better. Jim's mother never blessed their marriage or accepted Jim's wife.

Consequently Jim harbored bitterness toward his mother for all the cursing and criticism. Unbeknownst to Jim, this created patterns of expectancy in his heart that kept him tied to his mother deep inside. Without realizing it, he began to expect his wife to treat him the way his mother did. He expected her—and all women for that matter—to eventually criticize and reject him, even though his wife had never treated him that way. This was wreaking havoc in Jim's marriage because over time Jim began to force his wife into the same role his mother had played.

It was the unconscious fear of being criticized that caused Jim to default on all his domestic responsibilities. As a result, he had given his wife only three bad options:

1. Do nothing and watch everything around them deteriorate

2. Continue to nag Jim and try to get him to perform, usually with little success and great frustration

3. Give up and do it herself

Initially she waited for Jim to do what he promised. Yet eventually, in frustration, she began to criticize and nag him just as his mother had done. This made Jim even more determined to avoid doing anything for fear that he would do it wrong and be further criticized. Eventually, much to Jim's relief, his wife chose the third option to just do things herself. He thought everything was great, but she was frustrated beyond belief. Jim had forced his wife to be his mother instead of his spouse, inadvertently reproducing in his wife the same pattern of criticism and cursing his identity that he hated in his mother.

Until Jim could truly forgive his mother for constantly cursing his identity and then receive the Lord's blessing and impartation of his true identity and destiny, he would not be free to become one with his wife and be a proper husband to her. Once we identified Jim's root issue—the tie to his mother— Jim was able to break free from the judgment of his mom and the fear of failure. Much to his wife's delight, Jim was finally able to become the responsible husband God had created him to be. Many couples just like Jim and his wife have found tremendous healing when they realized that the root cause of their marital difficulties was that one or both of them were still tied to a parent who had not imparted his or her blessing.

Refusal to Release
Curses the Identity of Married Children

Another potential way parents can curse the identity of their married children is to not allow them to emotionally leave home. It is sometimes very difficult for parents to release their married children and allow them to be joined to a spouse. Even though they have blessed their child's marriage and received the marriage partner, they still want to make decisions for their married child. When this occurs, it is very important for the married child to set boundaries on what input he is willing to receive from his parents. He must also make sure his marriage partner is his first relational priority, not his parents.

Recently a father told me about an encounter he had with his married daughter. She called home one night crying and upset about an argument she'd had with her husband. They both had said some unkind things that they didn't mean, and now the daughter wanted to come home. This wise father told his daughter, "Honey, you are home. I will always love you, and you will always be my daughter, but your home is no longer here. It is now there with your husband." How difficult that must have been for a loving father to say to his hurting daughter! However, this wise father clearly understood his role to listen and comfort, but then to direct his daughter to the Lord and back to her husband to continue becoming "one flesh" with him.

FAMILY PARTNERSHIP STRATEGY FOR SELECTING A MARRIAGE PARTNER

I have spoken with many parents who were distraught over the person their son or daughter had married. I have also spoken to many people whose marriage has been very difficult or even ended in divorce, and often they tell me their parents did not approve of their choice of spouse. Only after some life experience—often around age forty—do they see the wisdom in their parents' caution. This is why is it so important for parents to be involved in the process of selecting their adult child's marriage partner.

As the old expression goes, love is blind. It can also be deaf, dumb, and stupid. When the blinders come on, the child in love may fail to notice negative character traits, generational patterns of sin, or family history that may affect a future marriage. For this reason that young person needs another set of "eyes" that are clear of any romantic attachment. The primary people God has placed in the lives of children to help them see more objectively are their parents.

I am not suggesting that we return to the arranged marriages common in biblical Hebrew culture. However, I believe there is a way for parents to be involved in their child's marriage selection process that is neither as restrictive as an arranged marriage nor as permissive as our current dating system in which the parents have very little input. I believe a more appropriate strategy would be a partnership in which both the parents and the children seek God together to discern who He is sending to be the child's spouse.

Using the powerful principle of agreement, this strategy prepares the child to function in agreement within marriage. Most of us who have been married for some time have made the mistake of making a decision our spouse did not support. In almost every case in my own life I wish I had listened to my wife. We discovered early in our marriage the principle of agreement. If only one of us thought we should do a particular thing, we found it was better not to act. Jan and I discovered that when we were in agreement about a decision, most of the time that was the will of God.

It is wise to teach children this principle of agreement when we are preparing them to be released into manhood or womanhood. During the time of instruction we can explain that we can best discern the will of God regarding their future spouse when all of us—both parents and kids—are in agreement. If only one of us thinks someone is the marriage partner sent from God but the other does not, there is a good chance that this is not God's plan. However, when parents and a child are in agreement about the person, the will of God likely will be found in this agreement.

When a family has walked this way, it is very easy for the parents to tell the adult child at marriage to apply the same principle of agreement in his relationship with his spouse.

There is also very little chance the parents will not bless the marriage.

In order to properly implement this partnership strategy, one must recognize the five principles upon which it is based:

1. The purpose of marriage is not to make one "happy" but to empower an individual to fulfill a destiny in Christ that he or she can better fulfill married than single.

2. God knows better than we do whom our son or daughter should marry, and He will bring His choice of a marriage partner into our child's life at just the right time.

3. Our child's heart and body do not belong to him to give away as he wills; they belong to God and are to be reserved in purity until marriage.

4. The will of God in a marriage partner is best discerned in agreement between the parents and child.

5. Both parents and child trust that God will use both parties to reveal His will despite their respective weaknesses and faults. This engenders mutual respect, honor, and trust in God.

When parents walk alongside their children in selecting a marriage partner, there is a much greater chance that the child will experience a successful marriage and fulfill with his spouse the purpose God has for his life.

What's So Wrong With
the Current Dating System?

Something is obviously wrong with a system that has roughly a 50 percent failure rate, but that is what our current dating system has produced. Nearly half of marriages today are ending in divorce.

For clarity's sake, when I use the word *dating* I am talking about the strategy in which a young person spends time with people of the opposite gender in hopes of developing a boyfriend-girlfriend type of relationship with someone special. In this dating relationship the two parties intentionally develop a mutually strong feeling of romantic love toward each other. This system is insufficient for managing romantic relationship and ultimately selecting a marriage partner. Let me explain why.

Dating inverts God's design.

God created people as three-part beings: spirit, soul, and body. The spirit should be subject to God, the soul (mind, will, and emotions) subject to the spirit, and the body subject to the soul. In dating, people are usually first physically attracted to someone, then emotionally, then possibly spiritually. By focusing first on the physical, God's order is inverted. In contrast, godly partnership allows the young person and the parents to first look for someone with godly character, then to consider emotional and physical attractiveness secondarily.

Dating focuses on self-gratification.

The unconscious motive for dating usually sounds something like this: "I want someone who looks physically attractive to *me* and makes *me* happy, someone *I* enjoy being with, who has interests similar to *mine*." The focus is on gratifying and pleasing self. In contrast, godly partnership would have the young person focus on blessing and serving someone else. The motive of relationship is self-sacrifice, not self-gratification.

The goal here is to lay down one's selfishness to serve another, not to use another to make oneself happy.

The idea is like a flea in search of a dog versus a rechargeable battery for a cell phone. The flea's goal is to *take* life from the dog. The battery's job is to *give* life to the cell phone. When the dog can no longer provide life to the flea, the flea abandons that dog and looks for another. When the battery runs out of life, it returns to the recharger (Jesus Christ) to receive more life so it can provide more life to the phone.

Dating has no long-term goal.

The primary purpose of dating is to "have fun." When the fun is over, the relationship usually terminates. Godly partnership allows the heart to go out in romantic love only to a person who both the parents and child believe is a potential marriage partner sent from God. The goal of the romantic relationship is to head toward the covenant of marriage.

Dating is often emotionally damaging.

When two fifteen-year-olds are dating, they do not usually have the goal of marriage in mind. They just want to have fun, but their hearts become fused together in romantic love for the duration of the relationship. This is like gluing two pieces of paper together. When one party no longer finds the other pleasing, the relationship breaks, but the hearts do not come apart the same way they went together. There is a ripping and tearing that cause significant emotional pain.

Each flea, I mean young person, then goes in search of another boyfriend or girlfriend to ease the emotional pain of the breakup. Each time a breakup occurs, the person leaves a piece of his heart with that individual. Suppose this happens five, eight, or ten times before marriage. How much of the heart is really left to give to a spouse? The heart often is so wounded the person needs massive emotional healing just to get back to the place God intended him to be at the start of marriage. If that healing does not take place, imagine the turmoil that will ensue when two wounded fleas marry each other!

In contrast, godly partnership seeks to reserve both the heart and body to be given only to the one God sends to be the marriage partner. In this strategy young people may spend lots of time together in groups, but they do not pair off as boyfriend/girlfriend and engage in romantic relationships with people they have no intention of marrying. The commitment of the son or daughter in this strategy is to preserve both the body and the heart (emotions) in wholeness and purity to be given only to a future husband or wife.

A young woman I'll call Sarah shared with me a powerful story. She was a Christian high school student who had been dating fairly regularly. One night she went out on a date to a movie with a young man. They kissed and hugged in the theater, and she thought little of it until a few days later when she was reading Proverbs 31, which tells of the godly woman. Verses 10–12 struck her in particular.

> An excellent wife, who can find? For her worth is far above jewels. The heart of her husband trusts in her, and he will have no lack of gain. *She does him good and not evil all the days of her life.*
>
> —EMPHASIS ADDED

Sarah told the Lord, "I want to be a godly woman as described here." Then she heard the Holy Spirit ask her, "So can the heart of your husband trust in you? Are you doing him good and not evil all the days of your life?"

She responded, "Lord, I don't have a husband yet. I'm only sixteen."

Back came the next question, "When does it say you should do him good and not evil?"

Sarah read verse 12 again. "All the days of my life," she mused. "I guess I am already in 'all the days of my life.'"

"Yes," she heard the Lord reply. "So are you doing your husband good and not evil?"

"Lord, I don't know. I don't know who my husband is."

"I do," the Lord replied. "Was that young man you went to the movies with your husband?"

"He's a nice guy," she said, "but I don't think I'd marry him."

"So he's not your husband?" queried the Lord.

"No, he will not be my husband," Sarah replied.

The Lord then told her, "Here's how you can tell if you are doing your husband good and not evil. What if the man who will be your husband had accompanied you on the date and observed your behavior with the other young man? How do you think he would have felt?"

Interjecting her future husband into the image of last week's date totally changed the picture. "He would have felt very betrayed and hurt, I suspect," she replied.

"Why?" asked the Lord.

"Because I gave someone else what should have been reserved for him," she said. "I get it. My kisses and my heart actually don't belong to me. They belong to You, Lord, for You to hold in trust until my wedding day, when I give my whole heart and body to my husband."

Sarah repented of treating her body as if it were hers to give away. She received God's forgiveness and then heard the Lord tell her, "Your heart and body do belong to Me, but your father is the human agent I have charged with guarding your heart and your body until your wedding day. On your wedding day your father will transfer the responsibility to protect you to your husband."

With this revelation Sarah never went on another date. A year and a half later she met the man who was to be her husband, and on their wedding day she was able to present him with a healed, whole, pure heart. To see the fruit of this kind of commitment, you may want to check out this short video clip of a bride on her wedding day returning to her father the purity ring he gave her when he blessed her at puberty and released her to become a woman: www .familyfoundations.com/index.php/dating15.

Dating is good preparation for divorce.

I have heard some people say they thought dating was good preparation for marriage. So the idea is that a relationship with no long-term goal, based on physical attraction and rooted in self-gratification, and that ends as soon as one person is no longer pleasing is good preparation for marriage? I think not! This is excellent preparation for divorce. This system teaches young people nothing about marriage, which is a lifelong commitment to God's purpose through unconditional, self-sacrificial, covenant love. Godly partnership is much better preparation for marriage. It helps teach young people to deny self and seek to bless others first.

Dating leaves virtuous young women to reject and fend off lustful young men.

God never designed a woman to do this. God has assigned a father the job of protecting his daughter's heart and virginity. When a father is not involved, a daughter must do this for herself. Unfortunately, since God did not design women to do this, she must harden her heart in order to continually say, "NO, NO, NO, NO, NO!" Do you think that a woman's disposition to protect herself emotionally and sexually instantly disappears on her wedding night? Of course not! This may negatively affect her sexual and emotional relationship in marriage for years.

Godly partnership, on the other hand, entails the father protecting his daughter. He is the door through which any young man must come. In this strategy the daughter has her dad screen any young man with romantic interest in her. The father will then grant or deny the young man access to his daughter's time or heart. Because she doesn't have to harden her heart and reject him herself, her heart can be soft and vulnerable when she gives it to her husband in marriage.

Dating usually does not involve the counsel and agreement of parents.

As I mentioned earlier, young people are blinded to the potential negative qualities of the person in whom they have a romantic interest. They need the benefit of another set of objective eyes, which parents can provide. Part of the consequence of this blindness is the near 50 percent divorce rate we now have in most Western countries. In contrast, partnership takes advantage of the parents' insight. This strategy allows romantic interest to develop between two parties only when both the parents and child are in agreement. The children commit in advance not to give their hearts to anyone until they and their parents are in agreement that the individual is a potential marriage partner sent from God.

Dating results in more marriages that parents choose not to bless.

Children brought up in the dating system usually don't ask parents before they enter into a romantic relationship. They usually announce only their intention to marry. At this point it is too late for the parents to have any valid input. Consequently parents are placed in the awkward position of being asked to bless something they don't approve of. In contrast, godly partnership involves the parents before any romantic relationship begins. In this strategy there is a much greater chance that the parents will bless the marriage, especially when it is implemented from the time of the blessing at puberty.

I highly suggest that you consider teaching your children the partnership strategy of managing romantic interests and potential marriage relationships from the time of puberty. This will ensure the greatest chance that you will be able to bless your children when they marry.

WHAT IF MY CHILD WANTS TO MARRY SOMEONE I DON'T APPROVE OF?

Heartbroken parents frequently asked me what to do when their adult child has announced plans to marry someone they don't think is right for him. They wonder if they should go ahead and bless the marriage even if they disapprove of the child's choice. I believe the parents' blessing is so powerful to facilitate a successful marriage that I would recommend blessing the union if it is not morally wrong or a violation of your conscience.

However, I believe that it is incumbent upon parents to tell their adult child why they think he should not marry the person he has chosen. After sharing their concerns, the parents should then allow the child to make his choice without manipulation or control. If he chooses to marry, then I believe it is best for the parents to bless the marriage and receive the child's choice of a spouse.

The caveat is this: "if it is not immoral or a violation of the parents' conscience." If the child has chosen to enter into a same-sex, incestuous, adulterous, or polygamous marriage, then it would not be possible for me as a parent to bless the marriage or attend the ceremony. Such a marriage is not only unwise and distasteful but also morally wrong. As a parent you can bless a son or daughter who is making an unwise choice or one with which you don't agree. But you cannot violate your moral convictions and bless a child's sinful or immoral choice.

I know a couple I'll call Sam and Sharon. They were faced with this very dilemma with their son, John. When John was a senior in high school, he had an adulterous affair with his youth pastor's wife. They ended the relationship soon after it was discovered, and John eventually spent a year out of the city. Yet when he returned to the city, the youth pastor's wife divorced her husband and began seeing John. Sam and Sharon were appalled, and they counseled their son to end the relationship.

He refused, and a short time later he announced that he was going to marry this woman. He wanted his parents to attend the wedding, but Sam and Sharon were in great turmoil. They loved their son, but they were convinced that John's marriage to the youth pastor's former wife would constitute adultery according to Mark 10:12 and Luke 16:18. After much prayer and many sleepless nights, Sam and Sharon concluded that they could neither bless John in his marriage nor attend a ceremony celebrating his adultery.

It broke Sam's heart to tell his son this news, but he and Sharon could not violate their own consciences. Sam made it clear to John that he and Sharon loved him deeply and accepted him as their son no matter what choices he made, but they could not attend his wedding. Sam and Sharon continued to maintain a relationship with John. Then about two years later John went to his father for counsel during a very difficult time in his marriage. In that meeting John thanked his father for standing for what he believed even at the risk of jeopardizing their relationship, and for continuing to love and accept him despite his choices. John acknowledged that his parents had been right all along. He now saw his choices from God's perspective and was humbled and repentant.

In the case of Sam and Sharon, not attending the wedding and not violating their conscience was the best way to minister to their son at that time. However, if a marriage is not immoral, after lovingly sharing your concerns with your adult child, it is better for you to bless your child's choice, even though you disagree with it, than to withhold your blessing. If the marriage is immoral, you cannot bless the union or the child and retain a clear conscience before God.

GOD'S PROTECTIVE MEASURES IN ANCIENT HEBREW CULTURE

As at all the previous critical times of blessing, God established practices within ancient Hebrew culture that ensured almost every child received his parents' blessing when he married. Four traditions and social norms stand out in particular:

1. Marriages were primarily arranged by both sets of parents and thus were always blessed.

2. Everyone in the society considered marriage a lifelong covenant, and sex outside of marriage was a capital offense.

3. The father was "the door" to his daughter's life and heart; therefore she did not have to protect herself from lustful young men.

4. Fathers taught their sons to protect, honor, and respect women, and society reinforced such attitudes.

As distasteful as an arranged marriage would be to our Western minds today, I believe that God implemented this strategy in biblical Hebrew culture because it was so important to Him that every marriage be blessed by parents. Remember, one meaning of "to bless" is "to empower to prosper." I believe God wanted to ensure that every marriage would be empowered to prosper.

In ancient Hebrew culture divorce was a rarity, and virtually no one cohabited. An honorable man would never approach a young woman he was interested in directly; he would approach her father because Dad was the door he must pass through to even speak with the daughter. Even in our Western culture fathers served this role until the turn of the twentieth century. In the 1800s it was still common for a potential suitor to first approach a young woman's father before he attempted to court her. This protected her from inappropriate suitors and lustful men.

Because of these four protective practices, virtually all marriages and marriage partners in ancient Hebrew culture were blessed by both sets of parents. Unfortunately, because these practices have largely been abandoned today, there is a significant chance that a marriage will not be blessed or may even be cursed by parents and thus disempowered from prospering.

••• BLESSING TOOLBOX •••

In the following section we will look at some specific actions you can take and prayers you can pray over your children to help establish a culture of blessing at the time of marriage.

ACTION STEPS

1. As parents, embrace the strategy of godly partnership rather than dating for the management of romantic relationships and marriage partner selection.

2. Teach your children this strategy of godly partnership at the time of puberty and walk with them in relationship throughout their teenage years.

REMEDIAL PRAYERS TO BREAK THE CURSE

If you did not approve of your adult child's marriage and spoke words to curse the marriage

1. Repent of being the devil's agent to speak his message into your child's life.

You can pray something similar to this:

Father, I recognize today that I was the devil's agent to send my child Satan's identity message at the time of his marriage. Lord, I spoke words of death rather than words of life over [your child's name]'s marriage. Today I renounce the sin of cursing my child's identity and marriage. I repent of doing so and turn completely away from it. I can't pay for my lack of blessing, but I recognize that Jesus Christ died to pay for my sin. Today I receive the blood of Jesus to pay for cursing my son/daughter's identity and marriage, and because Jesus Christ paid for this sin, today I receive Your forgiveness. Father, because You have forgiven me, today I forgive myself for cursing [your child's name]'s marriage.

2. Meet with your child and acknowledge that you did not bless his marriage and ask for his forgiveness.

I suggest that if both parents are available, you do this together. If not, do so by yourself. It is important for you to choose your own words, but you may want to say something like: "We now realize that God called us as parents to bless your marriage. We did not do so. Instead we spoke words of death over your marriage. God has shown us that in so doing we sinned against you. Can you find it in your heart to forgive us? [Wait for an answer.] If you would allow us, we would now like to bless your marriage."

3. Now bless your child, his spouse, and their marriage.

I suggest that you pray over your child and his spouse together. You may pray something similar to this:

Father, this day we accept the marriage of [your child's name] *and* [your child's spouse's name]. *We bless this marriage and declare that you shall prosper in your marriage and in every area of your life together. You shall fulfill your God-given destiny as a couple and shall find great fulfillment in accomplishing your purpose together. We declare that* [your child's name] *is a wonderful husband/wife and will be used by God to bless his/her wife/husband. We declare that you shall prosper in your relationship with each other. We declare that you both shall be quick to forgive and bless each other. You shall prosper in your physical health. The fruit of your womb shall prosper. Your children shall love God with all their hearts. We bless your work and your finances and declare that you shall prosper financially. You shall find great favor with your employer and your friends. This day we release you to leave your father and mother spiritually and emotionally and to be joined to your wife/husband to become one flesh in Christ. We love you, and this day we bless you. We bless* [your child's spouse's name], *we bless your marriage, and we release you to fulfill all that God has called you to accomplish as a couple, in the mighty name of Jesus Christ. Amen.*

If you realize you have not released your son or daughter emotionally

1. Repent before God of not releasing your son or daughter.

You may want to pray something like this:

Father, I recognize today that I have not emotionally released my child to be joined to his/her spouse. I recognize that this has hindered him/her from properly becoming one with his/her spouse. Today I repent of keeping [your child's name] *in emotional and spiritual bondage to me. I ask You to forgive me for not releasing him/her sooner. I receive Your forgiveness. Right now, in the name of Jesus Christ, I release* [your child's name] *to leave me spiritually and emotionally and to be joined to his/her spouse. I bless* [your child's name]*'s marriage and declare that these two shall become one flesh and shall prosper in Jesus's name, amen.*

2. Meet with your child and ask him to forgive you.

Again, I suggest that if both parents are available, you do this together. If not, do so by yourself. It is important for you to choose your own words, but you may want to say something like this: "We now realize that we have not spiritually and emotionally released you to be joined to your wife/husband. Will you please forgive us? [Wait for an answer.] We would now like to release you and bless you to be joined to your wife/husband."

3. Bless your child and his spouse now and their marriage together.

You may wish to speak a blessing over your married children like the one outlined above.

PREVENTATIVE PRAYERS TO RELEASE THE BLESSING

Bless your child on his wedding day to release him to be joined to his spouse and to bless his marriage. You may want to pray something like this over your child:

[Your child's name], *today on your wedding day we are so proud of you. God has prepared you for this day and for your life as a married man/woman. You have everything you need to be a wonderful husband/wife. Today, as your parents, we release you spiritually and emotionally and bless you to be joined to* [your child's spouse's name], *to begin a new family and to become one flesh in Christ. We promise to stand with you and to fight for your covenant of marriage all the days of your life. We pray God's richest blessing over your life together.*

For a daughter, you may wish to address the groom and release your daughter to him as his wife. The father may also want to say, "I have protected and covered [your daughter's name] in spiritual authority all of her life until this day. Today I turn that responsibility over to you. We charge you to love [your daughter's name], cherish her, to protect her, and provide for her, even as Christ does for His bride, the church. We promise to pray for you and your marriage regularly. We are delighted to receive you into our family and to call you our son-in-law."

A father may also want to affirm his son, telling him, "Son, on this your wedding day we are proud to call you our son. You are prepared in every way to be a great husband, to lead your family spiritually, emotionally, and financially. We have every confidence that you will succeed and prosper as a husband, a father, and a man."

You may then wish to declare the following blessing over your child and his or her future spouse:

We bless your marriage and declare that you shall prosper in every area of your life together. You shall fulfill your God-given destiny as a couple and find great fulfillment in accomplishing your purpose together. We declare that you will be used by God to bless your wife/husband. We declare that you shall prosper in your relationship with each other. We declare that you both shall be quick to forgive and bless each other.

You shall prosper in your physical health. The fruit of your womb shall prosper. Your children shall love God with all their hearts. We bless your work and your finances and declare that you shall prosper financially. You shall find great favor with your employer and your friends. We love you, and this day we bless you. We bless [your child's spouse's name], we bless your marriage, and we release you to fulfill all that God has called you to accomplish as a couple, in the mighty name of Jesus Christ. Amen!

Chapter 10

BLESSING YOUR PARENTS IN OLDER AGE

IN THE SEVENTH critical time of blessing the family roles reverse. In the first six stages of life the parents bless their children, but in this seventh stage the children bless their parents. Proverbs 31:28 says the children of the virtuous woman "rise up and bless her." This then completes the blessing cycle. After parents have blessed their children in the first six stages of life, it is a natural for the children to want to bless their parents in their older age.

Just as every son or daughter longs to hear a parent say, "I love you, and I'm proud of you," so does every parent long to hear similar words from his or her adult children. In chapter 1 I mentioned that the Greek word for "blessing" is *eulogia*, from which we derive our English word *eulogy*. Unfortunately, the only time most adult children speak powerful words of blessing over their parents is after they pass away. These words of blessing spoken at a funeral may be of benefit to the other family members but not to the parent. Parents need to hear words of blessing from their children while they are still living, so God can use the child to help answer the parent's key heart questions.

My mother passed away recently at age eighty-six. At her memorial service I was able to read again the same blessing I had spoken over her fifteen years earlier when I chose to publicly bless my parents at one of our annual Family Foundations International conferences. I was glad to be able to attend my mother's memorial service with no regrets in my heart, knowing that I had said everything I wanted to say and had completed the blessing cycle while she was alive.

Several years ago I attended a party my friend Paul was hosting to celebrate his parents' fiftieth wedding anniversary. Paul had been quite a scoundrel for much of his adult life and was in his mid-forties when he gave his life to Christ. Consequently his parents were very surprised when Paul said he wanted to host a party to honor them on their golden anniversary. After I shared with Paul the power of blessing, he had decided to read a written blessing to his parents at the party. Paul had also told his brother about the concept of blessing and had convinced him to write and read a blessing as well.

Being a fairly wealthy man, Paul spared no expense in celebrating his parents. Because his parents were of German descent, Paul rented a hotel ballroom, hired a German polka band, and provided a buffet dinner for two hundred of his parents' friends. After all the guests had eaten, danced, and talked for a while, Paul and his brother took the microphone and announced that they had something to say to their parents. Each son proceeded to read the blessing he had written as a tribute to their parents' life and marriage.

I watched the faces of the guests as Paul read his blessing to his parents. Most had tears running down their cheeks, and I could tell they each longed to receive a similar blessing from their own children. After Paul had finished speaking, I overheard several guests telling Paul's parents, "You are so lucky to have a son like that! You must be so proud of him."

Seeing this response made me realize again the power of blessing. This was something every older parent was designed by God to receive from his adult children. Unfortunately, because many parents did not bless their children in the first six stages of life, it does not occur to the children to bless their parents later in life. If your mom and dad are still living, you can change that cycle in your generation by blessing your parents.

KEY ROLE PLAYER

The children are the key people God uses to impart His message of blessing into the hearts of the parents. Adult children can send a powerful message of blessing or cursing to their parents in older age through their attitudes and actions.

KEY QUESTION TO BE ANSWERED

The key questions in the heart of an older parent that either God or Satan will answer are: *Am I still needed? Have I really accomplished anything of significance in my life?* I believe there are three attitudes children can display that will bless and convey value to parents in their older age. They are *acceptance*, *admiration*, and *appreciation*.

Satan wants to use adult children to tell older parents they are worthless and rejected. He wants them to hear, "You are not needed any more. You have outlived your usefulness and are now just taking up food, air, and water on the planet. You have accomplished nothing in your life. No one appreciates you, and no one will tell you thanks because your life has meant nothing."

God's message, of course, is just the opposite. He wants to use adult children to tell adult parents, "Thank you for all you have done throughout your life to try to help me succeed and prosper. I recognize that you gave up a lot of time, money, and energy to sow into my life. You are the most awesome dad/ mom that anyone could have. I so admire you for what you have accomplished in your life. We still desperately need your counsel and wisdom in our lives. We want our children to know you and to be able to receive your love and wisdom."

BLESSING AND CURSING PARENTS

Even if parents have had significant faults in life, God wants to use their adult children to impart His message of identity and destiny into their hearts in their older age. Whether or not your parents had the knowledge or inclination to bless you growing up, in order to honor the Lord and to break the cycle of cursing, it is important for you to bless your parents in their older age. Let's look at what blessing and cursing parents might include.

Blessing parents later in life may entail such things as:

1. The children writing a tribute to each parent conveying gratitude and respect and choosing a meaningful time to read and present it to their parents

2. The children giving their parents a place of true respect and honor in their hearts and conveying God's message that the parents are still needed and have value in their children's lives

3. The children conveying honor and respect to their parents in the presence of their own children and teaching the grandchildren to value and honor their grandparents

4. The children supporting their parents spiritually and emotionally through prayer, visits, and regular communication

Cursing parents later in life may involve

1. The children never writing a blessing for their parents and instead criticizing, demeaning, or conveying ungratefulness to their parents

2. The children giving their parents no place of respect in their hearts and conveying the devil's message that the parents are not needed and not valuable

3. The children ridiculing and disrespecting their parents in the presence of their own children and teaching their children that older people have no value

4. The children cutting off their parents and not visiting or communicating with them

POTENTIAL CONSEQUENCES OF BLESSING AND CURSING

When children fail to bless their parents, both the parents and children may be robbed of enjoying a rich friendship as mutual adults. One of the greatest pleasures in family life is for older parents to be friends with their adult children and impart into the lives of their grandchildren. However, if the adult children harbor resentment or bitterness toward their parents, both the parents and children are robbed of the friendship God intended.

Furthermore, an adult child's blessing could open an unsaved parent's heart to the Lord. Some adult children have told me it would be difficult for them to bless their parents because their parents are hard-hearted and probably would not receive a blessing. However, we have discovered that blessing opens the heart while cursing closes it. Most often the reason people close their hearts is that their identity was cursed and their emotions wounded at some point in the past. Many adult children have been shocked to see their parents respond positively when they shared their desire to publicly bless them.

I have also heard many adult children say they had presented the gospel to their parents for years, and it seemed to have no effect. Yet after they presented to their parents a formal letter of blessing, their parents began asking them about the Lord. Some have reported that even angry, bitter, crotchety old parents who had not been godly examples opened up and accepted Christ in response to the honor and blessing their children conveyed to them.

Thus a powerful consequence of blessing is that it may open an unsaved parent's heart to the Lord. On the other hand, a consequence of not blessing one's parents is that they may remain closed to the gospel. This is a very serious potential consequence and worth considering as you decide whether or not to bless your parents.

Another potential consequence is that children who do not bless their parents may never be blessed by their parents. Remember that a parent's blessing empowers one to prosper in adult life. When people understand that parents hold the key to releasing their children to prosper, they often want their parents to bless them. One of the most powerful ways to elicit blessing from your parents is to bless them first. When a person is receiving blessing, one of the most natural responses is for them to turn around and reciprocate the blessing. Many adult children who have chosen to bless their parents have subsequently reported that a short time later, sometimes even the same day, the parents asked if they could reciprocate and bless the son or daughter.

Children who refuse to bless their parents may hold resentment and bitterness toward their father or mother and thus dishonor their parents through their attitude. Again, Deuteronomy 5:16 says that when you dishonor your parents, your life will be shorter and things will not go well with you—you will not prosper—in the land the Lord your God gives you. Some adult children struggle to bless their parents because the parents abused or cursed them. However, the verse in Deuteronomy does not exempt those children from honoring their parents.

It does not say, "Honor your father and mother unless, of course, they have abused, mistreated, cursed, or abandoned you, or treated you with gross injustice." It simply says, "Honor your father and mother." Period. The consequences of honoring or dishonoring a parent are unqualified and directly correlated with the choice of the son or daughter, not the behavior of the parent.

The question then may arise of how to bless a parent who abused or mistreated you. Again, the key is to separate identity from behavior. This way you can accept and honor the person while rejecting and hating the behavior. If you fuse identity and behavior together in your mind, you will fall into one of two ditches. In your attempt to hate and reject sin, you will hate, dishonor, and reject the person who sins. Or in your attempt to love and accept the person who sins, you will love or accept the sin as well.

God always separates the person (identity) from the sin (behavior). In this way God can avoid both ditches and love, accept, and even die for the unrepentant sinner (Rom. 5:7–8) while hating and rejecting the sin. This principle is the basis of forgiveness. It is not possible to forgive an unrepentant sinner unless one can separate identity from behavior and hate the sin while honoring the sinner.

This is why the consequence for honoring or dishonoring parents in Deuteronomy 5:16 is unqualified. Honoring a parent is not dependent upon the parent's behavior but on the child's ability to forgive. Satan understands this principle well and works very hard to ensure that abused children never forgive their parents but instead dishonor their parents by retaining resentment and bitterness. This dishonor gives Satan authority to enforce the consequence stated in Deuteronomy—that their lives will be shortened and it will not go well with them.

If you have struggled to forgive your parents, I would highly suggest that you receive healing from the Lord. At our Blessing Generations Experience events we have seen many people healed of the emotional damage and lies that resulted from abuse, unjust treatment, or the lack of blessing at any of the first six critical stages in life. Trained ministers walk people through the process of forgiving their parents and receiving the blessing from God that they never received from their earthly parents. As a result, they are able to honor their father or mother and become God's agent to bless them in their older years.

God's Protective Measures
in Ancient Hebrew Culture

Again we see that in ancient Hebrew culture God made it very difficult for parents not to be blessed by their adult children in their older age. God placed the following two protective measures in that society to ensure the blessing and honor of older parents.

1. Older people in general and parents in particular were held in high regard and treated with great respect.

2. Adult children had a natural desire to honor and bless their parents when the parents had blessed them in the first six stages of life.

In ancient Hebrew culture older people were considered repositories of wisdom and experience to be treasured and respected (Prov. 16:31; 20:29). Jesus also spoke in Mark 7 about the responsibility of adult children to honor their parents by making financial provision for them in their older age (Mark 7:9–12).

In contrast, modern Western culture has largely lost respect for older people. Many are ridiculed and shamed. Parents frequently speak disparagingly about their older parents in the presence of their children, thus teaching their children that older people are not valuable and are unworthy of honor. In reestablishing a culture of blessing, it is important for us as parents to teach our children to respect and honor our elders.

I am not aware of a specific ceremony of blessing in ancient Hebrew culture for older parents. I believe the blessing and honor of parents was a natural part of daily life in families at that time. I believe it is appropriate to mark the blessing ceremony for older parents in a tangible way, much as my friend Paul did at his parents' golden wedding anniversary. However, we would do well to embrace a lifestyle of honoring and supporting elderly parents in our culture.

••• BLESSING TOOLBOX •••

The key action step is to write a blessing for each of your living parents and find a meaningful time to deliver it to each of them. This will help establish a culture of blessing in your family.

There is great power in a public declaration. In chapter 8 I wrote about the power of a public ceremony and father's blessing to release a boy to be a man and a girl to be a woman. Just as we have lost the value of ceremony in our modern culture, I believe we have also lost the value of public declaration. A public proclamation not only affects the individual it is directed to, but it also releases authority in the spirit realm. A godly public proclamation by someone with legitimate authority releases the Holy Spirit and angelic hosts to accomplish what has been proclaimed. On the other hand, a satanically inspired public proclamation releases demonic forces to accomplish what has been proclaimed.

At a wedding ceremony there is a public proclamation that two formerly single people are now husband and wife. The couple is then issued a certificate documenting the declaration of their marriage. This seals something emotionally and spiritually in the hearts of the couple and in the spirit realm, and it creates a public record documenting the declaration of covenant made.

When slavery was abolished in January 1863, President

Abraham Lincoln did not just stand and say, "All slaves are now free." He crafted a special document called the Emancipation Proclamation and had it publicly posted because he understood the power of a public proclamation to revoke demonic authority, establish God's kingdom purpose, and impart vision into the hearts of people.

With this understanding, I highly encourage you to take the time to craft a special letter of blessing to your parents who are still living. Then find a unique, meaningful time to publicly read and present it to them. Author Dennis Rainey has called this written blessing for parents a tribute.[1] I think this word is fitting. You may also want your children to be present when you present your tribute. This will demonstrate to your own children the value of honoring parents and showing respect for older people. This also will help create a family culture of blessing for the next generation.

HOW TO CRAFT A TRIBUTE TO YOUR PARENTS

In his excellent book *The Tribute* Dennis Rainey explains in detail how to write a tribute. I will not be as exhaustive as he is, but I will outline seven simple guidelines for writing a blessing for your parents.

1. *List everything your parent did right.* Many times in older age parents don't remember very many of the things they did correctly. Perhaps they only remember their sins, faults, and mistakes. Take this opportunity to remind them of the things they did well.

2. *List everything you appreciate about your parent.* Write some words to thank your mom or dad for these actions or attributes.

3. *List godly character qualities you have observed.* If your parents were not believers and you are struggling to think of godly qualities, pray, and the Lord will show you the intentions of your parents' hearts. If your father went to work every day and came home only to sit and drink beer in front of the TV, you can thank him for being consistent and providing for the family. God will help you see the godly qualities in your parent if you ask Him to show you.

4. *List meaningful (or perhaps comical) experiences you and your parent shared.* Every family has had meaningful experiences. Perhaps you went on a camping trip together and the tent collapsed in the middle of the night. Perhaps your mom or dad took some action that saved your life. The purpose here is to bless your parent for their participation in your life.

5. *Use your lists to craft a tribute thanking your parent for his life and declaring the good things your parent did and the significant impact he or she has had in your life.* After you have written a draft of the blessing letter, I suggest you take some more time to edit it. Don't worry too much about being grammatically correct. Just put it into a form that sounds like you.

6. *Personalize the tribute.* Make it reflect your personality, and then decide how you would like it to be permanently displayed (i.e., calligraphy on parchment, printed and framed, hand carved into wood, etc.). The point of this step is to formalize your tribute into a permanent record that can be displayed in a prominent location. I suggest that

you spend some money and make it a beautiful expression of your honor for your dad or mom.

7. *Choose a day that is special to you and your parent and publicly read and present your tribute to your parent.* You may wish to select a birthday, anniversary, Mother's or Father's Day, or any other day that would be significant to your parent. It doesn't have to be a holiday. It may simply be a day when you and your parents are available. If both of your parents are still living, you can decide whether to present tributes to each of them on the same day or at different times.

In the late 1990s my wife and I sought the Lord about when to publicly bless my mom and dad. We felt the Lord wanted me to make a public proclamation of blessing over both my parents at our annual Family Foundations International conference that year. During one of the sessions at the conference I read each tribute, thanking both of my parents for all they had poured into my life, and then I prayed for and publicly blessed each of them. I am including portions of the blessing I wrote and presented to my mother to give you an example of what a tribute might look like.

A Tribute to My Mother, Vonnie Hill

As she saw her son fly by the second story window in a parachute, Mom quickly excused herself from her phone conversation and ran outside to see what had become of him. Having found him to still be in one piece, save for a broken arm, she, at his request, ran out to rescue his new parachute from the tree, which had captured it. Many moms would be so shaken by such an experience that they would be angry at the son for such foolishness and glad for the parachute to be destroyed by the wind so as not to risk any more disturbance by its use.

Mom, thanks for always caring more about me as a person and about the things that were important to me than about your own fear, discomfort, and inconvenience. As I have grown in my own parenting, I have found that it is very difficult to provide for a child both the opportunities to learn and grow as well as the appropriate boundaries to keep him secure and safe from harm. You have always done an expert job at showing love, being concerned, setting boundaries, but not controlling, limiting, or smothering. Thanks for not removing opportunities from me when I made mistakes growing up.

Many people whom I meet have a selfish, controlling, overprotective mom in whose sight they could do nothing right. I thank God that I had you for my mom. I have always felt all my life that you were more concerned for me than for how I affect you.

Many wish that their mom were a godly woman that they could look up to, admire, and be proud of. My mom is.

Many wish that their mom would listen to their point of view. My mom does.

Many wish that their mom had taught them about God growing up. My mom did.

Many wish that their mom would let them go emotionally to cleave to a wife. My mom has.

Many wish that their mom prayed regularly for them. My mom does.

Thanks, Mom, for praying for me and my family every day. Thanks for letting me participate in all the activities that I did in teenage years without limiting me as a result of fear....Even though you and Dad didn't have a lot of Bible teaching in your early adulthood, you have always lived a consistently godly life. Thank you that your speech and conversation has always been pure and upright. You have been a wonderful model of the godly woman that is spoken of in Proverbs 31. I love you! Thanks, Mom, for loving me and being my mom. I'm so proud of you as my mom. God has made me a blessed man.

Your letter should reflect your heart toward your parents, your personality, and writing style. It is not as important how you express your blessing to your parents as it is that you do so. Don't try to make your tribute perfect; just write it and let it be a true expression of your heart.

Some people have expressed a concern to me that their father or mother would never allow them to read such a letter publicly. I have encouraged people with this concern to pray and ask for God's favor and the right timing to ask their dad or mom if they could bless them. Most are surprised by the openness they experienced when they prayed in advance and expected God's favor.

REMEDIAL PRAYERS TO BREAK THE CURSE

If you have cursed your parents in older age

1. Repent before the Lord of being the devil's agent rather than God's agent in the lives of your parents.

You may want to pray along these lines:

Father, I recognize today that I have been the devil's agent to send to my parent Satan's message in his older age. Lord, I spoke words of death rather than words of life over my dad/mom. Today I renounce the sin of cursing my parent's identity and of not granting him a place of honor and respect in my heart. I repent of the dishonor that has been in my heart and ask You to forgive me by the blood of Jesus Christ. Father, I pray that You heal my dad/mom from the damage I did through my attitude and words of dishonor and cursing of identity. I ask You now to bless my father/mother in older age. Lord, I ask You now to grant me favor with my dad/mom to find an appropriate time to go to confess my wrong attitude, ask forgiveness, and bless and honor my father/mother. Amen.

2. Meet with your father/mother and acknowledge your lack of blessing and ask forgiveness.

When you meet with your parents, it is important that you choose your own words and that you speak from your heart. You may wish to say something like this: "Dad/Mom, I have come to realize that my attitude toward you has been disrespectful, judgmental, and ungrateful. I now realize that this is wrong and that I have sinned against you through my attitude and actions. Could you find it in your heart to forgive me? [Wait for an answer.] I would now like to thank you for all you have done for me throughout my life and share with you some thoughts I have written down in preparation for this time together today."

3. In the same meeting, after you ask forgiveness, move into a time of blessing.

Read your letter of tribute and bless your father/mother.

If your parents abused or mistreated you and you are struggling to bless them

1. I encourage you to pray a prayer of forgiveness and healing similar to this:

Father, my dad/mom mistreated me and deeply wounded me. I realize today that I have protected myself against further wounding by establishing a protective barrier in my heart of resentment, bitterness, and blame toward my dad/mom. Lord, I have trusted in my own protective barrier rather than trusting in Your blood. Father, today I want to take down that barrier of resentment, bitterness, and blame. I repent of trusting in my own wall of resentment to protect myself, and today I ask You to forgive me.

I recognize that my dad/mom cannot pay for the way he/she hurt and mistreated me. But Jesus, You already paid for all my dad's/mom's sin against me. I declare today that Your blood is enough to cancel the debt in my heart against my dad/mom. Today I accept Your blood as full payment for my dad's/ mom's sin against me. Because You have paid, I declare today that my dad/mom doesn't have to pay any more. Because of Your blood, I forgive my dad/ mom. I now place my trust in You to protect me and keep me safe in the future.

I further realize that I have chosen to dishonor my dad/mom in my heart because of what he/she did and how I and others in my family were treated. Lord, I acknowledge that it was sin for me to dishonor my dad/mom. Today I repent of that dishonor toward him/her in my heart. I ask You to forgive me. Since I have forgiven my dad/mom for what he/ she did, today I choose to grant my father/mother a place in my heart of honor and respect. I choose to honor and bless my father/mother.

Lord, I ask You now to grant me favor with my dad/mom to find an appropriate time to confess my lack of honor, ask forgiveness, and bless and honor my father/mother. Amen.

2. I now suggest that you follow the previous steps and find a time to meet with your parents.
You may also want to attend a Blessing Generations Experience to find further healing and receive from your Father God the blessing you did not receive through your dad or mom.

If your mom or dad has already passed away and you did not bless them while they were living, you will not be able to bless them at this time.

However, I encourage you tell the Lord the things you would have liked to say to your parents. Do not speak directly to your parents, as the Bible forbids us to speak to the dead and calls this witchcraft (Deut. 18:11). However, you can exhaust your heart of things you would have liked to have said by speaking directly to the Lord. You then may wish to pray something like this:

> *Father, I did not take the opportunity to bless my father/mother and share my tribute while he/she was living. Lord, I recognize that I cannot pay for that mistake, and I ask you to forgive me by the blood of Jesus Christ that was shed for all my sins, mistakes, and faults. I receive Your forgiveness, and today I forgive myself for not taking the opportunity to bless my dad/mom while he/she was still living. Lord, I would have liked to have told my dad/mom these things:* [now is the time to pour your heart out to the Lord regarding the unspoken blessing of your parent(s)].
>
> *Father God, I recognize that I cannot continue to hold on to my dad/mom in my heart. I will always love him/her and cherish the memories I have. Thank You, Lord, for the time I had with Dad/ Mom. I recognize today that he/she really belongs to You, not to me. Therefore, today I choose to let my dad/mom go. I release him/her into Your hands, in Jesus's name, amen.*

PREVENTATIVE PRAYERS TO RELEASE THE BLESSING

Create a culture of blessing in your family by organizing a time to have a public proclamation of blessing to your father and mother if they are still living. Do this by following the action step above. After presenting your tribute, you may wish to proclaim a blessing similar to the one below. Drawn from *The Family Blessing Guidebook* by Terry and Melissa Bone, this was written by adult children and spoken over their Christian parents in their older age. You will want to adapt the language to suit your specific situation.

> We want to take this opportunity to honor and bless you for your character and virtuous deeds throughout your life.
>
> We honor you for the years of selfless service spent in raising your children, for providing for our material, emotional and spiritual needs.
>
> We honor you for preferring our needs over your own and for the sacrifices you made for our sake.
>
> We honor your commitment to following the Lord Jesus and bless you for imparting your spiritual values to us.
>
> We honor you for providing Godly role model(s) to follow. We are blessed and inspired by your integrity.
>
> We thank you for your many prayers that have guarded us from unseen troubles.
>
> We thank you for imparting your wisdom and teaching us valuable life lessons.
>
> We thank you for being available for us in the following ways: *(at this point in the blessing a couple of brief stories are shared).*
>
> For the remaining years that God grants you to remain upon the earth:
>
> May you never be without the presence of the Holy Spirit,

May your heart always be at peace,
May your mind always be alert and learning,
May your strength match the length of your days,
May God keep you in His love at all times.

We bless your memories that you may recall the goodness of God and the great times had with family and friends.

We bless your spiritual life, that you may continue to worship God in spirit and truth.

We commit ourselves to walk with you for the rest of your journey on earth.

During the sunset years of your life, as you become less able to care for yourself, we will become more available to help look after your needs...

Or if separated by distance... to visit when we are able and to pray for you when we cannot be near.

As you look upon your children today, you are also looking at the beginning of a legacy that will last for generations.

We commit ourselves to carry forward your legacy and pass on our spiritual heritage to our children and grandchildren.

The LORD bless you, and keep you;
The LORD make His face shine on you,
And be gracious to you;
The LORD lift up His countenance on you,
And give you peace.

—NUMBERS 6:24–26

Chapter 11

FAMILY BLESSING: THE KEY TO RECLAIM THE FAMILY MOUNTAIN

IN RECENT YEARS there has been a fair amount of discussion in Christian circles about reclaiming the seven mountains of culture. The concept is that in order to impact any nation for Jesus Christ, we must affect the seven spheres, or mountains, that are the pillars of any society: business, government, media, arts and entertainment, education, the family, and religion. In his 2011 book *Change Agent,* my friend Os Hillman observed that these seven spheres are controlled by a small percentage of leaders and networks. In fact, he wrote that it takes "less than 3–5 percent of those operating at the tops of a cultural mountain to actually shift the values represented on that mountain."[1] Os goes on to say:

> James Hunter, in a 2002 Trinity briefing, highlights what sociologist Randall Collins says about civilizations in his book *The Sociology of Philosophies.* According to Collins, civilizations have been defined by a very small percentage of cultural philosophers who influence seven gates and supporting networks since our birth as a civilization. Hunter summarizes, "Even if we add the minor figures in all of the networks, in all of the civilizations, the total is only 2,700. In sum, between 150 and 300 people (a tiny fraction of the roughly 23 billion people living between 600 B.C. and A.D. 1900) framed the major contours of all world civilizations. Clearly, the transformations here were top-down."[2]

Since the beginning, culture has been defined by a tiny fraction of the population—no more than three thousand people. "That is why we must realize that making more conversions will not necessarily change culture," Os writes. "It is important to have conversions, but it is more important to have those who are converted operate at the tops of the cultural mountains from a biblical worldview.... The more liberal and ungodly the change agents at the top, the more liberal and ungodly the culture. The more godly the change agent at the top, the more righteous the culture will be. It doesn't matter if the majority of the culture is made up of Christians. It only matters who has the greatest influence over that cultural mountain. *And the mountain of family must undergird all other cultural mountains.*"[3]

Indeed it is true that the family mountain is the foundation of all the other cultural mountains. Why is this? I believe it is because parents hold the power to either release their children to prosper and fulfill their God-given destiny or to hinder them from doing so. Many of our children are called to be key influencers at the top of the other six cultural mountains. However, if we as parents don't understand our responsibility to create a culture of blessing in our own homes and to multiply this culture within our communities, then many children will be hindered from prospering and fulfilling their destinies.

It is the power of a parent's blessing that imparts God's vision and confidence into children's hearts, releasing them to become key influencers at the top of the other six cultural mountains. However, in the last several decades we Christians have allowed a culture of cursing to take root in our society and consequently have steadily lost our influence even within the family mountain itself.

Unfortunately it is a fact that since the late 1960s those holding a biblical worldview have steadily been losing their influence over marriage and the family in North America.

Even as recently as the 1970s, if a couple had a long-term romantic interest in each other, most considered marriage to be their obvious next step. Once the couple decided to marry, even those who did not attend church or synagogue regularly would contact a pastor, priest, or rabbi to conduct the wedding ceremony and provide some premarital counseling.

That is hardly the case today. Many couples who are romantically and sexually involved may not even choose to get married, and those who do may never consult a pastor or religious authority to perform the ceremony. In reality, biblical Christians are not the primary influencers guiding society's standards regarding romantic, sexual, and family relationships. We have been seriously losing the battle for this influence, as Os Hillman indicates with the following statistics.

> Over the last forty years, marriage has become less common and more fragile, and the proportion of children raised outside intact marriages has increased dramatically. Between 1970 and 2008 the proportion of children living with two married parents dropped from 85 percent to 66.7 percent, according to census data. About three-quarters of children living with a single parent live with a single mother.
>
> These important changes in family structure stem from two fundamental changes in US residents' behavior regarding marriage: increases in unmarried childbearing and high rates of divorce. More than a third of all US children are now born outside of wedlock (39.7 percent), including 71.6 percent for African American babies and 27.8 percent for whites and other ethnic groups.[4]

> "Sixty-five percent of young adults whose parents divorced had poor relationships with their fathers (compared to 29 percent from non-divorced families)," according to a study on family life released by sixteen of the top scholars on the importance of marriage.[5]

The *Washington Times* described the impact of divorce on children. "More than half of American teens have grown up with parents who 'rejected each other,' which bodes ill for the nation's future leadership, productivity, wealth, and well-being, says a new national report on American families. Only 45 percent of teens aged 15–17 have grown up from birth with their married, biological parents, says the new US Index of Belonging and Rejection."[6]

In previous chapters we have looked at the serious spiritual and emotional consequences of being conceived outside the protective hedge of marriage. The above statistics tell us that over 70 percent of African American babies and nearly 40 percent of all babies born in America find themselves with little blessing and no protective spiritual hedge at conception and in the womb. This means that most of these children will receive a powerful impartation of Satan's message of identity and destiny through their parents right from the beginning of life. Some may even be attacked by demonic spirits in the womb.

Unless there is supernatural intervention, the enemy will have free rein to plant a deep-seated feeling of rejection and worthlessness in the hearts of these children. If that happens, these children will desperately need an impartation of blessing to break the power of the curse in their lives. Without a powerful experience with Jesus Christ to exchange Satan's message for God's, these children will almost certainly repeat the same family patterns of their parents.

We have also looked at the desperate need for fathers to be involved in their children's lives, particularly at puberty. As we have seen, it is the blessing of the father that releases a boy spiritually and emotionally to be a man and a girl to be a woman. The statistics above tell us that only 45 percent of all children will still have both parents at home through the teenage years. This means that more than half of all children would not even have the chance of being blessed by their fathers and released into their adult identity when they reach puberty.

Why Christians Are Losing the Battle for the Family

I believe the primary reason we followers of Jesus Christ have lost our influence over the family mountain is that we do not have much of a culture of blessing in our own families. Honestly, it is no more likely that a person who grew up in a Christian family would have been blessed at the seven critical times of life than someone who grew up in a family professing no faith. Yet receiving blessing at the six critical times of life is the foundation that empowers a child to develop a healthy identity and sense of destiny. In their own search for value, love, and purpose, children who grow up without the benefit of a parent's blessing tend to embrace the same destructive values promising short-term gratification as those in the society around them.

Embracing such values has led to the same statistics concerning divorce, affairs, premarital sex, teenage pregnancy, substance abuse, and emotional/behavioral disorders among those who grew up in Christian families as those from families professing no faith at all. This has led the world around us, and even children of churched parents, to ask the legitimate question, "Why would we want what you have in your family? Your 'faith-based' family life produces no better results, and in some cases you produce worse results and more dysfunction than we do."

This should be a wake-up call for us because the criticism is not without merit. Something is wrong. In recent decades we have not been change agents in influencing the family mountain.

We previously talked about the prophetic admonition from the Book of Jeremiah to "stand by the ways and see and ask for the ancient paths, where the good way is, and walk in it; and you will find rest for your souls" (Jer. 6:16). Blessing in the seven critical stages of life is an ancient path. When families practice this ancient path of blessing, it really does bring rest to the souls of children.

Children who have been blessed by their parents tend to be at peace inside, having a secure sense of value and purpose. Adult children who have never been blessed by their parents are frequently not at rest inside and tend to spend much of their lives seeking value and purpose through their performance and relationships. Such adults are not free to love a spouse from a place of security in their own value. Rather, they look to a spouse to make them feel valuable.

The lack of peace in a person's soul caused by the absence of parental blessing often sets families up for generational cycles of divorce and dysfunction. I described this cycle in a message I gave at our Family Foundations International annual conference in 2010.

> Divorce and remarriage in one generation deeply wounds the hearts of children and sows the seed of insecurity, shame, and performance orientation into the next generation. When these wounded children grow into adulthood, such seed then frequently reproduces in marriage the fruit of one or more of the four "Big As": adultery, abuse, abandonment, or addictions.
>
> These symptoms then in turn result in divorce in the second generation. If core issues are not dealt with in marriage, and true healing is not brought to the deep wounds of the heart, but rather we continue to accept divorce and remarriage as an appropriate solution to these four "Big As," we can expect an intensification and proliferation of ever-increasing deviant sexual sin in each succeeding generation. Gay marriage is just the tip of the iceberg of things to come. History records that just

such a cycle ultimately led to the downfall of the Roman Empire. If we hope to avoid repeating Roman history ourselves, our priority must be the authentic healing and transformation of hearts in this generation, and the restoration of the family in our nation and in the world.

Unfortunately in much of the church today divorce and remarriage are considered acceptable solutions when a spouse manifests one or more of the four "Big As." It is my opinion that most leaders are not taking stock of the generational and societal consequences of this policy. Many church leaders seem to feel that somehow these four "Big A" issues are beyond the power of God to heal. However, just as Jesus set free the Gadarene demoniac in Mark 5:1–20, He can likewise heal, set free, and send home husbands and wives who have been bound by adultery, abuse, abandonment, and addiction.

A discussion on how to bring true healing and restoration to both parties in a serious marital crisis involving these "Big A" issues is beyond the scope of this book. However, there are many other excellent resources on this topic. To start with, you may wish to read my book *Two Fleas and No Dog: Transform Your Marriage From Fleadom to Freedom.*[7]

When the enemy successfully ravages a marriage through adultery, abuse, abandonment, or addictions, faithless Christians often encourage divorce rather than healing and restoration for both parties. Unfortunately divorce breaks God's protective hedge of covenant in marriage and opens the door to the enemy to impart his message into the hearts of the children. I believe this is one reason many children of divorce receive a deep-seated irrational belief their parents' breakup was somehow their fault. The enemy also will use divorce to plant deep feelings of abandonment, guilt, shame, and perfectionism in children, who fear being permanently rejected the way they saw one parent cut off the other.

God designed marriage to be an unconditional covenant

based on grace. Divorce presents it as a conditional contract based on works or performance. Thus divorce distorts in the heart of the child the prophetic image of how Christ will treat us, His bride (Eph. 5:31–32). Instead of being a grace-based, unconditional covenant, marriage is seen as a performance-based, conditional contract in which an errant party can be thrown out and replaced with someone else who will perform more satisfactorily.

Divorce opens the door for the enemy to deposit his identity message into a child's heart and rob that child of peace in his soul. The perfectionism and need to control born out of shame causes children of divorce to potentially struggle with guilt and depression in adulthood. The children in adulthood may then attempt to soothe their deep feelings of worthlessness, abandonment, guilt, and shame with alcohol, drugs, pornography, sex, and other addictions. These symptoms of anger, control, depression, alcoholism, drug abuse, pornography, and sex addiction all then manifest in the adult children's marriage relationships as the same adultery, abuse, abandonment, and addiction that caused their parents to divorce in the first place.

Now we have one or more of the same four Big As in the second generation, which again lead to divorce, and the cycle repeats itself in greater intensity in the third generation. In some generation God's people must recognize that *divorce and remarriage are not the solution to the four Big As in marriage. Rather, they are the seed to produce the four Big As in the next generation.* In order to turn this generational cycle of cursing into a generational cycle of blessing, someone, somewhere, sometime will have to choose to die to their own personal short-term benefit and choose instead to live for the long-term blessing of their children and future generations (Mark 8:34–37).

However, this does not mean that a spouse who encounters any of these four Big As is just to accept such behavior and do nothing. While divorce is not the answer, it is very important for a spouse facing emotional, sexual, or physical abuse to immediately (at the first occurrence) report this situation to his/her pastor or spiritual authority and seek help for the family (1 John 1:7).

Family cycles of abuse are rarely, if ever, resolved without help from outside the family. God never intended for a spouse to deal with abuse in the family in isolation by herself/himself. Together with the counsel of your pastor you must quickly design and implement a plan to protect yourself and other family members who may be in danger and to confront the abuser and get him/her the necessary help. This plan will probably include the assistance of counselors, specialized ministries, and perhaps civil authorities.

The choice of a spouse to die to the short-term temptation to permanently terminate marital relationship through divorce and rather to remain committed to the long-term healing and restoration of the marriage is one of the most potent prophetic images of the gospel that can be portrayed. It is not too hard to love one who loves you, to bless one who blesses you, to be faithful to one who is faithful to you. But to be faithful to one who is not faithful to you, to accept one who is rejecting you, to bless one who is cursing (abusing) you—this is a little harder and is the true prophetic image of what Jesus Christ has done for us (Eph. 5:28–32).

EXCHANGE OF THREE KEY VALUES IN SOCIETY

I mentioned earlier that Christian children who have not been blessed tend to embrace the same short-term values as the society around them. It is this value exchange that has caused Christians to lose influence over the family mountain in society. I have seen three key values exchanged over the last several decades, first in society and now also in much of the church.

218

1. The Word of God as an absolute standard of truth has been exchanged for the Word of God as a relative standard.

2. Self-sacrifice as a virtue has been replaced with self-gratification as a virtue.

3. Marriage as a covenant has been exchanged for marriage as a contract.

I believe the enemy has been able to perpetrate the exchange of these three values primarily because we have departed from God's ancient path of blessing at the seven critical stages of life. As we have seen, blessing brings a person's soul into rest and causes him to feel secure, loved, and valuable. People who have not been blessed tend to live with emotional pain and great insecurity. This frequently motivates them to seek short-term self-gratification instead of sacrificing in the present to reap benefits down the road in their own lives and in future generations.

Let's look briefly at these three values. As a follower of Jesus Christ, I hold a deep belief that the Bible is the inspired Word of God. It is the product of handpicked men who spoke and wrote as the Holy Spirit inspired them. Consequently I accept the Bible as my infallible source of truth. This means that I grant the Bible authority to govern what I believe and how I live. If there is a conflict between the written Word of God and a circumstance, feeling, prophetic word, dream, experience, or counsel of a pastor or leader, I choose to value the written Word of God above any other subjective word or experience.

However, in recent decades, especially with the advent of modern science, people have been taught to doubt everything until it is proven tangibly. As a result, people no longer see the Bible as an absolute standard of what is right and truth but as a relative standard that must be tested and proved like anything else. The problem with this strategy is that many people are perishing as they experiment with violating God's ancient paths. Unfortunately many do not discover the consequences of violating scriptural principles until after tremendous damage has been done, not only to themselves but also to their children and future generations.

I am continually amazed when Christians tell me they have decided to pursue a course of action directly opposed to the Bible's clear instruction. When I ask why they think this is the right choice, they often cite a prophetic word, dream, vision, circumstance, or bit of advice that led them to this decision. Subjective words and experiences must never supersede God's Word.

To understand the consequence of this value exchange, imagine a lighthouse being situated on a moving vessel instead of in a fixed location. Ships that rely on the lighthouse to help them navigate through treacherous waters will crash on the rocks because there will be no stationary reference point to help them find their way. Their guidepost will be constantly moving. This is exactly what is happening to many families in the church.

The second value that has been exchanged is self-sacrifice for self-gratification. Self-sacrificial living was once a deeply held value among Christians. After all, Jesus sacrificed His life for us. In Genesis, when God told Abraham that He would bless and prosper him, it was not only for his benefit. All the families of the earth would be blessed through Abraham.

Historically families lived, ate, and worked together. That is how they survived. If one person refused to carry his responsibility, the whole family could suffer or even perish as a result.

Today corporate physical survival has been replaced by individual emotional survival. Each person carries so much emotional damage that the goal for many is to simply survive and, as much as possible, avoid further emotional pain. This way of thinking, of course, retains the individual in the emotionally immature state of dependence, making him reactive instead of proactive. Such a person is then kept as a victim of circumstances and the choices of others, which continues to generate abundant emotional pain.

One of the primary results of this value exchange is that children who grew up in this environment have lost their intrinsic sense of worth. In times past each person growing up felt unique and special. He felt valuable to God and to society, as though he were here for a purpose far greater than himself. I recently read a letter my father wrote to his dad in 1945, explaining his plans after the war. My father grew up in a traditional denominational church and at that point in his life did not have a strong sense of being led by the Lord. Yet note the values he held as a twenty-year-old man.

> After the war I plan to return to school to study many different scientific, military, and political fields. My main interests lie in the many fields of science such as medicine, genetics, physics, chemistry, astronomy; and certain scientific, psychological, mental effects connected with medicine. The only reason that I would go into politics or military affairs is if they are as corrupt as they have been so many times in the past. That is, if we win the war and lose the peace so as to find ourselves in just as bad a position as if Germany had won the war, then it would seem necessary to go into a political war against these darn political ring leaders that frequently run our congress. In my case I don't give a darn about money. As long as I can get enough to eat and a little clothes to wear, I will spend the rest of the time wherever it can do the most good, *whether it's fighting international military wars or fighting political ring leaders or trying to lick some baffling scientific problems.*

What shocked me most was the sense of purpose my father possessed as a twenty-year-old. He definitely valued self-sacrifice above self-gratification. He wanted to be of service to his countrymen, have enough food and clothing to live, and then spend the rest of his time wherever he could do the most good. After I read this letter, I asked my father if he'd had an unusual attitude as a young man. He told me he was not unique. Most of his friends and classmates had a similar outlook.

This value of self-sacrifice has all but disappeared from our present society. What's worse is that many Christians have lost it too. For a follower of Christ, happiness is not the true goal of life. It is to expand and promote the kingdom of God. Joy and fulfillment are by-products of serving Jesus. Anyone who seeks the by-product rather than the goal misses out on both. Jesus said, "If anyone wishes to come after Me, he must first deny himself, and take up his cross and follow Me. For whoever wishes to save his life will lose it, but whoever loses his life for My sake and the gospel's will save it" (Mark 8:34–35).

So serving Jesus and serving self are incompatible goals. One is based on self-sacrifice, the other on self-gratification. God doesn't force us to serve Him; He gives us the choice. Which path we take—service or self-gratification—depends on the values we truly hold. If you want to dig deeper into this particular value exchange, I explored this topic at length in my book *Help! My Spouse Wants Out.*[8]

The third value that has been exchanged in our society is that of marriage as a covenant; many people now see it as a contract. Before the 1960s most people in society and virtually all church leaders believed marriage was a lifelong covenant that depicted the grace-based relationship between Christ and His church (Eph. 5:31–32). In most churches the wedding vows included a line that went something like this: "I, John, take thee, Jane, to be my wedded wife, to have and to hold from this day forward, for better or for worse, for richer, for poorer, in sickness and in health, to love and to cherish, till death us do part, according to God's holy ordinance; and thereto I plight thee my troth."

To "plight a troth" is to give something in pledge. So you see, those vows are the words of a covenant, to be terminated only by death.

A contract and a covenant are two entirely different concepts. A covenant can be characterized as unilateral, unconditional, and irrevocable. It is best described as a promise that shall not be broken, terminated only by death. A contract, on the other hand, is bilateral, conditional, and revocable. It is an agreement completely dependent upon the performance of either party and terminated by the default or betrayal of either party. As you can see, these are completely different concepts.

What's more, a covenant is dependent upon the *word* of the one who made the covenant. A contract, however, is dependent upon the *works* (performance) of the relevant parties. While a covenant is based on self-sacrifice, grace, and forgiveness, a contract is based on self-fulfillment, works, and justice.

A contract is like a sales transaction. If I agree to sell John a car for $10,000, I don't have to give him the car if he gives me only $5,000. I am released from the contract and am free to sell the car to someone else if John doesn't fulfill his word.

A covenant, on the other hand, is like an irrevocable promise. If I promise to give John my car because I love him and want to bless him, the fulfillment of my promise is not dependent upon anything John does or does not do. John's receiving the car is dependent only upon my integrity to keep my word. Even if John becomes angry with me, lies about me, betrays me, and tries to destroy me, I will still give him my car because I gave him my word that I would. This is a covenant.

Does your relationship with Jesus Christ more resemble a covenant or a contract? I hope it resembles a covenant. It is not dependent upon your works but upon His Word. If you sin against Him, betray Him, or become addicted to substances or sinful habits that are an abomination to Him, Jesus does not terminate relationship with you, kick you out, and replace you with someone else. His relationship with you is a covenant, dependent on His promise, not your performance.

God designed marriage as a covenant and deposited it on the earth to depict the relationship between Christ and His church. Unfortunately the enemy has all but eradicated any prophetic image of how Christ treats His church through our exchanging marriage as a covenant for marriage as a contract.

Many couples still vow, "Till death us do part," during the wedding ceremony, but they live as though their marriage is a conditional contract. They will accept and authorize the permanent termination of the marriage (divorce) and replace their spouse with someone else (remarriage) if one of the four Big As (adultery, abuse, abandonment, or addiction) manifests in their marriage. I have told some pastors, "If you believe marriage is a contract, then please stop leading people to lie in the wedding ceremony by using the covenant language 'till death us do part.' It would be better to change your language to say what you truly believe: 'I take you to be my lawfully wedded husband...till adultery, abuse, abandonment, addictions, or death us do part.'"

PRACTICAL STEPS
TO CREATE A CULTURE OF BLESSING

As we have looked at each of these seven critical times of blessing in some detail, we have seen that in ancient Hebrew culture it was almost impossible not to be blessed at each of these stages of life. In our modern Western culture it would be rare for someone to have been blessed at even a few of the critical stages of life. I believe we can change that, and in one or two generations your children and grandchildren will be able to say, "I grew up in a culture of blessing. My parents blessed me in all six of the critical stages of life. Wasn't that the case for everybody who grew up in a Christian family?"

We can create a new generation of young people like John Quincy Adams or Betsy Ross, young men and women who have a settled sense of identity and purpose from a very young age. This new generation who has grown up in a culture of blessing will be secure enough to uphold values that will benefit all of society and future generations. Why not let these world-changers be your children and grandchildren?

Let's now look at what you can do practically as one family to create a culture of blessing and become a change agent to help regain influence in the family mountain in our society. If you are married, it is best to implement these steps as a couple. If you are a single parent, you can implement most of these steps on your own.

For the steps that cannot be implemented alone, look to godly family members and to the body of Christ to stand in the gap with you for your children. You can trust God, your Jehovah Jireh, to always provide what you need at just the right time. Let's now look at the steps you can take to create a culture of blessing in your family.

1. Determine to create a culture of blessing in your family and in your community by blessing your friends, neighbors, and coworkers.

2. If you are married, make a regular habit of praying together as a couple daily and speaking a blessing over each other.

Remember to look into your spouse's eyes as you pray, and take one minute each for repentance and forgiveness, thanksgiving, and blessing.

3. Receive ministry to be healed of past cursing of identity.

Our Blessing Generations Experience offers this kind of ministry. It empowers people to receive healing from past cursing and receive blessing from their heavenly Father if they were not blessed by their earthly parents. It also prepares participants to bless their own family members during each of the seven critical stages of life.

4. Begin to separate identity from behavior when relating to and disciplining your children.

Bless your children's identity even when you must apply a consequence to discipline their behavior. Remember the principles in chapter 2 about communicating clear expectations to your children, planning discipline in advance, and being quick to repent and bless your child if you make a mistake.

5. Develop a regular habit of having a Sabbath meal together as a family once a week.

Speak a blessing over each of your family members, following the tips in chapter 3 about how to do so.

6. Consider becoming a change agent by inviting one other family to dinner on your family blessing night.

After you bless your own family members, ask your guests if you can bless them also. If they ask, teach them how to conduct their own weekly time of blessing. In this way you can help begin a blessing revolution in your community.

7. Embrace and use the power of blessing at the seven critical stages of life.

Bless your children at the *time of conception.*

 Pray to break the power of past cursing your children may have experienced at conception.

- Bless the conception of your current children.

- Prepare an environment of blessing for your future children.

Bless your children during their *time in the womb*.

- Pray to break the power of past cursing your child may have experienced while in the womb.

- Bless any current children whose identity you cursed or failed to bless in the womb.

- Bless your unborn children every day they are in the womb.

Bless your children *at birth*.

- Pray to break the power of past cursing your child may have experienced at birth.

- Bless any current children whose identity you cursed or failed to bless at birth.

- Have a ceremony of blessing for your newborn roughly eight days after birth to publicly dedicate the child to the Lord. Declare the meaning of the child's name, affirm his/her gender identity and destiny, and share any words the Lord has given you for your child.

Bless your children *during infancy and early childhood*.

- Pray to break the power of past cursing your child may have experienced in infancy and early childhood.

- Bless any current children whose identity you cursed or failed to bless during infancy and early childhood.

- Bless your children regularly during infancy and early childhood.

Bless your children *at puberty* and release them into their adult identities.

- Pray to break the power of past cursing your child may have experienced during adolescence.

- Plan and conduct a bar/bat barakah-type of blessing ceremony to release your son/daughter into his/her adult identity. Do this at the time of puberty, but if you missed that opportunity, plan a ceremony regardless of your child's age. Remember to include the three key components: instruction and preparation, ceremony, and celebration.

Bless your children at *the time of their marriage.*

- If your children are already married and you did not bless their union, as long as the marriage was not immoral, repent and bless the marriage and your child's spouse now.

- Develop a family strategy for managing romantic relationships and the marriage partner selection process before your children reach puberty. I suggest the strategy of godly partnership between parents and child rather than the traditional dating system. Teach your children your family strategy for managing relationships as they reach puberty.

- When your adult child marries, publicly proclaim your blessing over the marriage at the wedding and release your adult child to be joined to his/her spouse.

Bless your *parents in their older age.*

- If you have cursed your parents in their older age, ask God to forgive you.

- Find a time to bless your living parents with a public tribute. Have your children join you.

- If your parents are not yet in their latter years, plan in advance to bless them. You may wish to ask your children and siblings to join you.

When we first begin to understand how far our Christian culture has strayed from God's ancient path of blessing, it can be a bit overwhelming. However, I suggest that you move forward using the proverbial strategy for eating an elephant: take one bite at a time. Just pick one new habit to implement at a time. I suggest that you sequentially follow the steps outlined above. Start by deciding to establish a culture of blessing in your family. Then if you are married, begin to pray with your spouse and bless each other daily. Once this habit is in place, move on to step three. Then begin to plan and implement a strategy to bless your children as you discipline. When this is working well, move on to step five and so forth.

I would also encourage you to follow the first command God ever gave man in the Bible, "Be fruitful and multiply" (Gen. 1:28). In the Bible Joshua motivated an entire nation to return to God's ancient paths by making a personal declaration. He said in essence, "I don't know what you want to do. You have to make your own choice whether you will serve the Lord God or the idolatrous gods of the nations. *But as for me and my house, we will serve the Lord."* (See Joshua 24:15.) Revolutions are started by contagious people who infect those around them with their passion. Once you begin to build a culture of blessing in your own family, intentionally start inviting other families into your home and infect them with your virus of blessing.

So how do we as followers of Jesus Christ become change agents and win back our right to influence the family mountain of society? We initiate a family revolution of blessing one family at a time. Parents who are blessing their children produce blessed families. Blessed families intentionally blessing other families produce blessed communities. Blessed communities blessing other communities produce blessed cities, which ultimately produce blessed regions and nations. Authority and influence in the family mountain of society can once again be restored to the church—if each family understands, implements, and shares with others the power of a parent's blessing.

Notes

Introduction

1. Biblesoft's *New Exhaustive Strong's Numbers and Concordance with Expanded Greek-Hebrew Dictionary.* Copyright © 1994, Biblesoft and International Bible Translators, Inc., s.v. *"barak,"* OT:1288.

2. W. E. Vine, *An Expository Dictionary of Biblical Words* (Nashville: Thomas Nelson Publishers, 1985), s.v. *"berakah,* to bless," OT:1293.

3. Ibid., s.v. *"eulogeo,* to bless," NT:2127.

4. Ibid.

Chapter 2
Creating a Family Culture of Blessing

1. John Trent and Gary Smalley, *The Blessing* (Nashville: Thomas Nelson, 1993), 30.

2. *Fiddler on the Roof,* directed by Norman Jewison (1971; Hollywood, CA: MGM).

Chapter 3
God's Ancient Path: Seven Critical Times of Blessing

1. Steven Silbiger, *The Jewish Phenomenon* (Lanham, MD: M. Evans, 2009).

2. Ibid., 2.

3. Ibid., 4.

4. National Park Service, "John Quincy Adams Biography," http://www.nps.gov/adam/jqabio.htm (accessed December 7, 2012).

5. Nancy Spannaus, "Ben Franklin's Youth Movement: Making the American Revolution," *Executive Intelligence Review,* December 15, 2006, http://www.larouchepub.com/other/2006/3350bens_youth_mvmt.html (accessed December 7, 2012).

6. Noel and Phyl Gibson, *Evicting Demonic Squatters and Breaking Bondages* (Drummoyne, Australia: Freedom in Christ Ministries Trust, 1987).

CHAPTER 4
BLESSING YOUR CHILD AT CONCEPTION

1. Centers for Disease Control and Prevention, "Unmarried Childbearing," September 14, 2012, http://www.cdc.gov/nchs/fastats/unmarry.htm (accessed December 7, 2012).

2. For more detailed information on the biblical Hebrew culture, you may wish to read Alfred Edersheim's classic book on the subject, *Sketches of Jewish Social Life in the Days of Christ* (London: The Religious Tract Society, 1876).

3. National Marriage Project at the University of Virginia and the Center for Marriage and Families at the Institute for American Values, *The State of Our Unions 2009*, http://stateofourunions .org/2009/SOOU2009.pdf (accessed December 7, 2012).

CHAPTER 5
BLESSING YOUR CHILD IN THE WOMB

1. Craig Hill, *If God Is in Control, Then Why...?* (Littleton, CO: Family Foundations International, 2008).

2. Thomas Verny with John Kelly, *The Secret Life of the Unborn Child* (New York: Simon and Schuster, Inc., 1981), 12–13. Used with permission of Simon & Schuster, Inc., and Lowenstein Associates, Inc.

3. Ibid., 15.

4. Ibid., 22–23.

5. Ibid., 18–19.

6. Ibid., 25.

7. Ibid., 26–27.

8. Ibid., 30–31.

9. William Wilson, *Wilson's Old Testament Word Studies* (McLean, VA: Macdonald Publishing, n.d.), s.v. "rasha."

10. Blue Letter Bible, "Lexicon Results: Strong's H2114—*zuwr*," http://www.blueletterbible.org/lang/lexicon/lexicon.cfm?Strongs =H2114&t=KJV (accessed December 10, 2012).

11. Blue Letter Bible, "Lexicon Results: Strong's H8582—*ta'ah*," http://www.blueletterbible.org/lang/lexicon/lexicon.cfm?Strongs =H8582&t=KJV (accessed December 10, 2012).

12. For more information on attending a Blessing Generations Experience near you, visit www.familyfoundations.com.

13. Verny, *The Secret Life of the Unborn Child*, 65.

CHAPTER 7
BLESSING YOUR CHILD IN INFANCY AND EARLY CHILDHOOD

1. Kim Knight, "The Consequences of Sensory Deprivation in Early Childhood," *The Art of Health*, July 14, 2010, http:// kimknight101.wordpress.com/2010/07/14/the-consequences-of -sensory-deprivation-in-early-childhood/ (accessed December 10, 2012).

CHAPTER 8
BLESSING YOUR CHILD AT THE TIME OF PUBERTY

1. Craig Hill, *Bar Barakah: A Parent's Guide to a Christian Bar Mitzvah* (Littleton, CO: Family Foundations International, 2011).

2. Robert Lewis, *Raising a Modern-Day Knight* (Carol Stream, IL: Tyndale House Publishers, 2007), 103–104.

CHAPTER 10
BLESSING YOUR PARENTS IN OLDER AGE

1. Dennis Rainey, *The Tribute* (Nashville: Thomas Nelson, 1994).

2. Terry and Melissa Bone, *The Family Blessing Guidebook* (Burlington: I.D. Ministries, 2012), 188–189. Permission to quote requested.

CHAPTER 11
FAMILY BLESSING: THE KEY TO RECLAIM
THE FAMILY MOUNTAIN

1. Os Hillman, *Change Agent* (Lake Mary, FL: Charisma House, 2011), 8.

2. James Davidson Hunter, "To Change the World," *The Trinity Forum Briefing*, vol. 3, no. 2, 2002, http://www.ttf.org/pdf/Bv3n2 -Hunter-Text.pdf (accessed April 5, 2011), as referenced in Hillman, *Change Agent*, 8.

3. Hillman, *Change Agent*, 8–9, emphasis added.

4. Institute for American Values and University of Virginia's The National Marriage Project, "The State of Our Unions: Marriage in America 2009," December 2009, as referenced in Hillman, *Change Agent*, 117–118.

5. Institute for American Values, *Why Marriage Matters: Twenty-Six Conclusions From the Social Sciences*, second edition

(New York: Institute for American Values, n.d.), as referenced in Hillman, *Change Agent*, 118.

6. Cheryl Wetzstein, "Majority of Teens Live in 'Rejection' Families," *Washington Times*, December 15, 2010, as referenced in Hillman, *Change Agent*, 118.

7. Craig Hill, *Two Fleas and No Dog* (Littleton, CO: Family Foundations International, 2007).

8. Craig Hill, *Help! My Spouse Wants Out* (Littleton, CO: Family Foundations International, 1995), 45–54.

About the Author

CRAIG HILL AND his wife, Jan, give senior leadership to Family Foundations International, a nonprofit Christian ministry through which they conduct life-changing Ancient Paths weekend experiences in forty-eight nations of the world.

Through his past experience in business, missions, counseling, and pastoral ministry, Craig has gained unique insight into marriage, family, generational, financial, and interpersonal relationships. By interweaving personal stories with biblical truths, Craig is often able to pierce through the veil of the mind to minister to the depths of the heart, resulting in authentic life change for many. Craig is the author of many books. He and his wife live near Denver, Colorado.

For information on Ancient Paths Experiences taking place near you; a complete catalog of other books, DVDs, and CDs by Craig Hill; or a listing of Craig's speaking schedule, visit:

www.familyfoundations.com

Or if in the United States, call (303) 797-1139

EMPOWERED
TO RADICALLY CHANGE
YOUR WORLD

Charisma House brings you books, e-books, and other media from dynamic Spirit-filled Christians who are passionate about God.

Check out all of our releases from best-selling authors like **Jentezen Franklin**, **Perry Stone**, and **Joseph Prince** and experience God's supernatural power at work.

**CHARISMA
HOUSE**

www.charismahouse.com
twitter.com/charismahouse • facebook.com/charismahouse

FREE NEWSLETTERS
TO HELP EMPOWER YOUR LIFE

Why subscribe today?

- ❏ **DELIVERED DIRECTLY TO YOU.** All you have to do is open your inbox and read.

- ❏ **EXCLUSIVE CONTENT.** We cover the news overlooked by the mainstream press.

- ❏ **STAY CURRENT.** Find the latest court rulings, revivals, and cultural trends.

- ❏ **UPDATE OTHERS.** Easy to forward to friends and family with the click of your mouse.

CHOOSE THE E-NEWSLETTER THAT INTERESTS YOU MOST:

- Christian news
- Daily devotionals
- Spiritual empowerment
- And much, much more

SIGN UP AT: **http://freenewsletters.charismamag.com**

8178